HE
CARRIED
A SPEAR

ALLAN LARSON

ISBN 978-1-09839-679-4 (Print)

ISBN 978-1-09839-680-0 (eBook)

CONTENTS

CHAPTER 1

NEW BEGINNING

The lions were roaring the morning he was born. Their roars resounded across the brushy country of southern Africa announcing to all that this area belonged to the Nyati Pan pride, other lions not welcome. The distant elephant herd was not concerned; a roaring lion is not a hunting lion. The lions they couldn't hear concerned them much more, for lions would attack young elephants if given the opportunity.

All the elephants in this small herd of nineteen seemed to sense that an event was at hand. For Njeri, the young mother to be, this would be her first calf. It had been growing inside her for twenty-two months and her time was near. All the elephants in this herd were related: sisters, aunts, daughters, granddaughters, cousins, young sons. No adult bulls were tolerated at this time.

The little band was patiently waiting in a grassy opening among scattered, thick-branched marula trees. The end of the rainy season, late March, was at hand and a gentle rain had fallen during the night. Wet leaves and grass glistened in the rays of the low morning sun. Steam rose off the backs of the wet elephants who appeared almost black on the side away from the sun.

The expectant mother was affectionately touched by many trunks as she patiently waited for whatever it was that was soon to happen. Often one of them would put her trunk into Njeri's mouth and she would do the same in return. The youngest elephants played and chased each other like giant puppies in the warming sun, unaware that anything unusual was about to happen. And then it did happen. Njeri paused amid the shuffling giants, uttered a low rumble, and as her stomach muscles tightened, she sighed, and the baby began to appear. Her legs bent and 250 pounds of brand-new elephant slid gently to the grass. The first-time mother was confused, although her instincts told her that this new life was hers to care for and protect. Almost immediately, the older cows were beside her nuzzling the baby, cleaning him, gently stroking him with their powerful trunks, showing Njeri what to do.

He lay without moving for several moments until the gentle rubbing and stroking of the experienced cows had him breathing deeply and struggling to roll over onto his stomach. Then, at last, he was on his feet, wobbling, staggering but upright, and he took his first hesitant footsteps. Then, he fell. He fell twice more, but each time, with a little help, he was able to struggle to his feet again.

He was a tired little fellow, but a new feeling was slowly emerging. At first, he didn't know what it was, but subconsciously he must have become aware that he was hungry. Somehow, both he and Njeri seemed to know what to do. With her trunk, she guided him slowly up between her front legs where her milk sacs were. He felt along her flank with his limp little trunk and clumsily tried to nurse. But his trunk was really his nose, not his mouth and it kept getting between his mouth and mother's milk. Her nipples pointed slightly outward, so standing a bit to her side, his mouth under his trunk finally made contact and he started to suckle. At first, he coughed and gagged; it was the first thing that had ever been in his mouth. Soon he was drinking easily as Njeri relaxed her muscles. It was all very new to her too.

Although he weighed 250 pounds, he looked tiny and vulnerable amongst the giants of the herd as he shuffled under his mother's belly. Dark hair covered his chunky body, and he carried his little trunk so that it seemed strangely short. His big ears were pinned to his sides and his black eyes appeared large for the size of his head.

Let him be Bahati, the Swahili word for "noble".

It was soon clear to the herd that all was well, and most of the herd moved off a bit and resumed feeding, but not before touching Njeri and Bahati tenderly with their trunks.

All was calm with the breeding herd, now numbering twenty, until two large hyenas appeared. They had come along a narrow trail through the brush, and the elephants did not see or smell them until they were only 20 yards away. But the elephants knew the hyenas to be opportunistic hunters as well as scavengers, and that the birth of a baby was full of potential for them.

This, however, was not to be the hyenas' day. Elephants are fiercely protective of their young and today hyenas would not be tolerated near them. Ears outstretched like sails, trumpeting wildly, the two young bulls that were still with the herd charged the hyenas at full speed. Strangely, the hyenas acted as though they had not expected this, and the bulls were on them almost before they could turn to run. A thick leg crashed into one and he was knocked to the ground and both of the young bulls were over him. He was instantly crushed beneath their great saucer-shaped feet. After worrying about the remains of the hyena for a few seconds, the bulls retreated and the herd moved slowly into the nearby mopane forest, the baby shuffling along beside the mother.

As night fell, the Nyeti Pan lions resumed calling and this time received a distant answer from a neighboring pride. The roars from the Nyeti Pan lions came from a pair of brothers and they knew the lion who was calling back. They had briefly scuffled in the past along the territory boundary. There would be no fight tonight; the brothers were eight-year-olds, massive mature males and the answering calls came from a single, younger lion who commanded a small pride of two lionesses and three cubs. His return calls were not a challenge; in two or three years, they would be.

CHAPTER 2

THE HONEY GUIDE

A small, well-muscled, barefoot man walks quietly beneath the shade of the mopane trees. A strap across his right shoulder carries a woven reed bag, which hangs on his left side. The bag holds only a small axe, a fire starter, a bit of wire, a few strips of biltong and a stoppered gourd full of water. His right hand carries a slender shaft of unusual design. It looks like, and is, a walking stick, but one end of it is split into many thin prongs about a foot long. Above him flits a small, chattering, grey bird. The man, Azaan, is a honey hunter and the bird is an African Honey Guide.

The man and the grey bird share a bond, a partnership that has endured for hundreds, maybe thousands of generations between man and bird. In exchange for small portions of the honeycomb, the portions with the bee larva, the honey guide leads the hunter to the hive. If the bird leads the hunter to the hive and the hunter leaves nothing for the honey guide, it is believed that bad things will happen to the hunter. Maybe the next time, the bird will lead the hunter into a bad snake or a lion or a buffalo. Azaan has never cheated his small partner.

The morning air is calm, the dew heavy, and the barefoot man moves almost silently. The forest is a dangerous place, and he wants to be able to hear what the forest sounds will tell him about what is ahead of him. He has hunted and taken what the forest would give him for more than twenty years. His wife tends a small garden by the big river, but she and the three children depend on what he is able to bring home. It is two full days of walking to get to his favorite honey area where the honey has a slight cinnamon taste. It is a long walk, but the man is as much at home in the quiet forest as he is in the noisy village.

The honey guide chatters incessantly and urges him to move faster. But he knows the hive is not going to move and the bird will stay with him; he moves ahead quietly and cautiously for more than an hour. The dew is nearly dry when, far ahead, he hears a branch break, then another. The honey guide is insistent on heading on toward the noise; but the barefoot man follows slowly, pausing often to listen. Soon he can hear the familiar low rumbling sounds of the elephants. All his life, he has lived around elephants and he senses that these elephants are agitated; they seem louder than usual, moving around but going nowhere, not eating. The air is still and the ground still damp and quiet, as he approaches, shielding himself behind trees and termite mounds. Then, Azaan sees the newborn calf and the dead hyena.

A slight breeze on the back of his neck tells him that he is in a most dangerous situation. He immediately drops his bag and stick and climbs quickly up through the thick, low branches of a close marula tree. When he is safely out of reach of the largest elephant's trunk, he looks out at a small clearing in the forest. Njeri stays away from the group with her baby beneath her belly while the adult cows confront the two "teenage" bulls. Elephants communicate with each other far better than most, maybe all, other land animals, but much of their vocalization is below the frequency level that the man in the tree can hear. It was, however, obvious to him that the big cows were telling the young bulls, who were as tall as the cows, that their boisterous behavior, their temper tantrums and unruliness were no longer compatible with the herd of cows and calves. They were clearly telling the young bulls to leave. They would, of course, have to be told a few more times, but they would leave and begin life with other bulls. Some would ally themselves with older bulls, in an association that may last for years. Some would form into small age groups of young elephants. It is the way with elephants.

Neither the elephants nor the small man noticed the big male leopard lying on a horizontal marula branch at the edge of the clearing. Had he seen it, Azaan would have been concerned, as he knew he would be walking many miles toward home in the dark.

When the breeding herd moved off, the man climbed down from the tree and was pleased to see that the honey guide was still there, chattering even more excitedly. Within thirty minutes, the bird hovered by a thick old tree. Fifteen feet up was a five-inch hole, stained dark below and buzzing with bees. The bird had done his job well; now it was time for the man to do his.

With the axe, the head of which that his village blacksmith had forged from an old truck leaf spring, he cut several sort-of straight trees and bound them together by cross pieces of the same wood, tied together with his wire and supple vines. He worked quickly and the shaky ladder reached to the hole. He had done this many times before and had occasionally fallen from his ladders when they slipped or collapsed, but he was never badly hurt.

Then, with the fire starter in his pouch, he built a small fire of grasses and sticks, and when it was burning well, put on a thick chunk of wet, rotten wood. When the wood was smoking heavily, he fitted it into the split ends of his walking stick, wrapped a rag around his face, and gently climbed his wobbly ladder. The excited bird flitted right above his head.

The bees attacked as he approached the hole, but they clearly didn't like the heavy smoke. When he reached the top of his ladder, he used his axe to open the hole wider, and then he dropped it to the ground. He next thrust the smoking stick into the hole and bees and smoke began to pour out. In a few minutes, only smoke was coming out and he reached in for the sticky combs. It was a rich hive and he dropped many, but not all of the combs into his bag. He thought he might come this way again and wanted the bees to rebuild. The man gingerly descended and tossed his ladder into the bushes for possible future use. Wire was valuable, so he took that back.

He had been stung many times, but he rubbed all that he could reach with a thick sap-dripping leaf, which his tribe had used for millennia, and the pain soon mostly went away. Sitting on the ground, he opened his bag and sat out on some broad leaves the parts of the combs with the most bee larva for the honey guide. He hoped that he and the bird would work together again.

The evening cooled as the sun dropped behind the trees. Later, as the sun fell below the horizon, a brilliant full moon rose in the east. The game trail that Azaan followed was long, but well-worn and dusty and, tonight, well lit. If he wandered off the trail a bit, his bare feet told him. The leopard watched him pass but did not move to follow. He would remain in the marula tree to guard and feed on his impala kill, which was stashed above him in the fork of a thick branch.

It was a long walk back to his home and late on the second day of his return trek, he heard a stick snap along the trail, far behind him, and later something coarse brushed against a dry bush; this time the sound was closer. He knew the sounds of the forest well and these sounds were unusual for the forest's quiet time. Then, he remembered the grey louries, the "go away bird" from the first morning. Several minutes after he had glided past them along the trail, something startled them and they called out raucously, "Go away, go away".

A dark, quiet forest is a good place for a man to think, to gather his thoughts, to listen. Azaan began to believe that he had not been alone today; he believed that he had been followed by an unknown someone or something. The men from his village would never spy on him, especially at night. It could have been a leopard or an antelope, but it wasn't, and he knew it.

CHAPTER 3

THE PAN

The game trails radiate out from the pool of water in the Nyeti Pan like the spokes of a wheel before disappearing into the surrounding brush. One trail, the one heading due east-west across the pan, is wider than the others. It is the one favored by the many small elephant herds. The big animals' eyesight is poor, and as they often prefer to go to water in the late afternoon, the trail puts the lowering sun at their backs, cutting down the glare and allowing them to know who or what is already at the water.

The last part of the game trail is a nearly straight line to the water. It is August, late in the dry season. Thirsty elephants, who have not drunk since the previous afternoon, often begin to trot or run when the life-giving water appears. Some race right in, some drink from the bank. After a long, hot dry day, if happy is an elephant emotion, they seem to be happy elephants.

Three hundred yards away, at the edge of the brush bordering the pan, the Nyeti Pan lion pride dozes in the late sun. Their bellies are full, and they are content, but they notice everything that comes to the water hole.

Earlier in the afternoon, the pride was slowly heading toward the Pan down the wide east-trending elephant track. The lions came out of the dry grass and scattered brush on the south side of the track and were walking single file toward the water. Seven heavily muscled adult lionesses led the procession, followed by two younger but fully grown lionesses, all trailed by six trotting cubs. They made no sound as they walked the dusty trail. The pride's two big males were continuing their siesta nearby.

Uphill from the lions, in the heavy brush on the north side of the trail, there was a slight noise from movement through the brush and dry leaves. The lions plodded on, but as the noise got closer and louder the pride switched abruptly from casual walkers to serious deadly hunters. Buffalo! Two of the trailing lionesses left the pride and headed uphill into the brush while the rest continued along the trail. The two quietly reached a place above a herd of 40 cape buffalo. They wanted their strong lion smell to drift down to the buffalo.

The pride lions were experienced, proficient buffalo hunters and the tactic was well understood by all the adults. When the lion scent reached them panicked buffalo thundered downhill through the thick brush, emerging on the game trail, right into the midst of the five killing machines with able assistants.

There were several young buffalo with the herd, but the lions attacked a big cow with long, slender horns. Nearly always lions first attack the rear end of the buffalo. As one of the lionesses on the trail hung onto the skin above the buffalo's tail, one of the big lionesses from the flanking pair crashed out of the brush and leaped onto the buffalo's back. Dragging one lion and carrying the second, the powerful buffalo charged into heavy brush and was able to shake off both lions and rejoin the stampeding herd.

But the cow was injured and tired and the lions sensed it. The hunt was not over. They caught up with the now-walking buffalo herd within half a mile. Instantly, they spotted the injured cow and attacked her right in the center of the herd. It was pandemonium but the lions were focused. The terrified buffalo herd scattered briefly, leaving the injured cow behind, alone. This time three heavy lionesses were able to force the buffalo to the ground. Another lioness seized the buffalo's throat and a fifth placed her mouth over the mouth and nose of the doomed cow, slowly suffocating it. Several times, bulls from the herd came back and short-charged the lions. The lions did not move; they were determined to keep their kill and the buffalo bulls seemed to know it.

Almost immediately the cubs were on the scene, in the scene with the adults, acting as though they had been a vital part of the hunt. As the adults began to feed, the cubs chewed hopelessly at the thick skin. Only after the big girls had peeled back some of the thick hide could the cubs begin to eat. They had learned a bit of the lessons of the hunt and the rewards, but not yet the dangers.

Less than an hour later, the two pride males appeared, quickly scattering lionesses and cubs and assumed prime feeding positions. The males seemed to be more tolerant of their own cubs than the lionesses were. Eventually, they all found a position on the carcass and began to eat their fill. In only a couple of hours, 1200 pounds of buffalo is reduced to hide, hooves and bones. The hyenas and vultures would process these meager remains.

Late in the afternoon, on the day of the buffalo kill, Njeri's herd looks down on the Nyeti Pan. A small breeding herd of elephants is already there, drinking at the east end of the water hole, but when they see the approaching herd, they began to leave. Their thirst satisfied, they slowly plod up one of the meandering trails across the pan opposite the resting lions.

As Njeri and the others pass the site of the buffalo kill, past experience and the elephants' extraordinary olfactory sense tell them exactly what happened three hours earlier. Now, they perceive no danger, no imminent threat.

The mud around the retreating water in the pan is baked hard. The deep footprints of elephants, cape buffalo, giraffes and rhinos made when the mud was soft, create a treacherous landscape for animals. Bahati is only four months old, so the hard-baked mud supports him on his four big flat feet. The adults in the herd reach the water by a smooth trail flattened by the passage of thousands of huge, heavily loaded feet.

Beyond where the hard-packed trail runs into the water, the mud is soft and sticky. Bahati has been here before and should know this, but in his thirsty excitement he runs off the hard surface, into the water. He has only recently figured out his floppy little trunk, and he greedily sucks water into it, and then squirts it into his mouth. Most of the water spills and he stands for a long time trying to get his fill. When he is finally satisfied, he turns toward Njeri, but he can't move. All four feet are firmly stuck in the dark mud. He is frightened, then terrified. His piercing baby shrieks shatter the quiet of the rapidly darkening evening.

Njeri wants to help her little boy, but the deep mud worries her. Her legs are so powerful that she can move in the mud, but she fears getting deeper. She trumpets in dismay. The herd quickly recognizes what has happened, loud rumblings of concern sweep the group.

The matriarch has seen this before, seen it here. She remembers that below the eighteen inches of sticky mud that holds Bahati, is a layer of firm sand. Her great weight pushes big feet quickly through the mud as she strides past Njeri to the frightened Bahati. She plunges her trunk into the muddy water and under him. He is over 500 pounds of dead weight stuck in the mud, but the buoyancy of the water helps her easily lift him and she guides him to the firm ground at the end of the trail. Eighteen inches of mud may doom a young elephant and scare bigger ones, but the immensely powerful female knew she could walk out of it and a frightening problem was quickly solved.

On the hill to the south, at the edge of the brush, in the last warm rays of the setting sun, the lion pride watched. They weren't hungry, but the potential of 500 pounds of some of their favorite meat was not to be ignored. As the elephants moved slowly along a narrow trail leading into the brush, a herd of about thirty impalas moved down to drink from a grassy bank a few inches above the water. As they often did, Nyeti Pan lions roared at sundown, letting other lions know that this land was taken. Or maybe they were just clearing their throats.

CHAPTER 4

MORGAN

The boy is seven and the old man, who is his grandfather, has entered his seventh decade. They are best of friends. The old man is Morgan. The boy is from the city and there he is called Samuel. His grandfather calls him Kitafe because he is small and dark and very quick like his Swahili namesake, the mongoose. He was always smiling and laughing, and this causes the old man to smile and laugh too.

The old man had lived his entire life in the bush. The things he and the other villagers grew within their small gardens and what they harvested from the forest and river had always sustained them. They had little need for money except for the few incidentals like sugar, oil, salt and tobacco and they usually traded for those. He was tall and lean, spoke slowly in a deep mellow voice. For many years, he had worked as a tracker for a famous professional big game hunter.

His true name incorporated the "clicks" of the Ndebili people and was nearly impossible for "others" to pronounce. One of the professional hunter's (PH's) American clients thought he looked like a well-known American named Morgan. So, the tracker became Morgan or Mr. Morgan to the clients from then on. He did not mind, but he wondered who this American Morgan was.

His tracking skills were unequalled. Other PH's tried to hire him away with more money, but he hardly needed any money, and he liked the old hunter and his hunting ethic. Morgan stayed with the hunter until the old man died and the hunting business passed on to a son. Then Morgan, the old tracker, went home to sit by the fire and smoke his pipe. He could not read or write, but his knowledge of the bush could have filled volumes.

The old man and how he lived was the reason Kitafe's parents in the city had sent him to live in the bush with his grandparents. Kitafe's parents were both born and raised in a bush village before circumstances forced them to the city. The culture and lifestyle of the bush ran deep in them and they wanted Samuel (Kitafe) to experience it before the city culture seized him forever. They wanted their only son to have a choice of cultures, a choice of values and to know this fine, old man.

One bright morning, toward the end of the dry, cool season, Kitafe walked over to Morgan's little house to sit with the old man in front of a small fire. It was a chilly morning in the small highland village.

"I see you Kitafe," he said in Swahili.

"I see you, honored elder," the boy replied.

They sat facing each other on log stools. The boy from the city said, "there are no wild animals where I live. Only dogs and some goats. I would like to see the wild animals, especially the elephants. Have you seen an elephant, grandfather?"

The old man smiled and, in his deep voice, slowly said, "Yes, I have seen them, many of them, many times. This is their home. But they are not here now."

"But you said that they live here, that this is their home."

Morgan smiled; the boy was not rude, just excited and happy to hear what the old man was saying. "It is now near the end of the long, dry season. The water they have been using here on the plateau has mostly dried up. They are now going to the big river, far to the north; it is the only water, and these elephants go to it every year. They need to drink a lot of water every day, but they also just like to be able to get into it. You would like to see them playing with each other and swimming and spraying water from their trunks."

Morgan's words created a vivid image in Kitafe's mind. He had a thousand questions, but he tried to hold back a bit. He knew he needed to be respectful. He knew that none of his city friends would ever have the conversation he was having with his grandfather. He thought he was entering a new exciting world. "Will we be able to see them, or must we wait until they return?"

"We will talk to your grandmother, but I think perhaps we should go to the river and see them there."

The next morning, the man and the boy were again on their stools in front of the fire. It was smoky around most of the other villagers' fires. Morgan's fire did not smoke. "Lottie," the old man said, "is concerned and a bit worried about an old man and a boy going so far and being alone amongst the animals. She is somewhat consoled, knowing that we can stay with Azaan, my son, who is your uncle, lives in a village on the river."

Three days later, they were packed and ready to leave for the Great Zambezi, four walking days to the north. Kitafe had little to pack; a few, very few extra shorts and tee shirts, a plastic raincoat, a blanket, and his toothbrush; it all fit easily into his city school backpack. Morgan's pack was sort of the same, but he carried matches and a fire starter and some food stuffs, cornmeal, biltong, salt, packed into an aluminum cooking pot. He had spent many years living off the land, in the brush, and he was anxious to show Kitafe that way of life.

Before he left Lottie and the little house, the old man picked up his spear. His father had given it to him at his coming-of-age ceremony, as his father before him had given one to him. Both would carry their spears all their lives and would be buried with them. Morgan had given one to Azaan at his ceremony and he earnestly hoped that the tradition would not be totally lost before Kitafe received his spear.

"I will lead us but…"

"But what?" interrupted a worried Kitafe.

"We are going to the bush, not a circus or a zoo. These animals are wild, and some can be dangerous." Morgan began in his deep, most serious voice, the voice that held a seven-year old's most rapt attention. "You will see many different animals, but the elephant is special, and not just for his huge size, big ears and wondrous trunk. With few exceptions, they are honorable, respectful and have a dignity rare in animals. She, not he, is a good family member. They are caring, extremely intelligent and furiously protective of their young. The bulls, the males, on the other hand, live in a different world than those of the breeding herd. The fine family attributes of caring and concern appear to be largely lost on the older boys. Parenting responsibilities are left to their passing acquaintanceships, and they spend most of their lives with the boys. They may never see or know their offspring. But don't judge them on human terms. This isn't good or bad; it is just the way it is and always has been with elephants.

Morgan, who had been standing, sat down on his log stool and lit his pipe.

In his most serious, seven-year-old voice, Kitafe replied, "I want to see them and hear them, and I would like you to teach me all that you know about elephants."

It was a better answer than the old man had expected, and he was pleased with the boy and anxious to show him the wild bush that he knew so well.

CHAPTER 5

THE LONG WALK

They left on a cool, foggy morning, headed north on a trail the old man knew well. He carried his few things in a cloth pouch sewn to a leather strap over his right shoulder. He carried his spear as a long walking staff in his right hand. At the end of his staff was a foot-long metal spearhead that the village blacksmith had fashioned from a piece of scrap metal. Kitafe had watched him sharpen it on a piece of flat sandstone, and knew it was sharp, deadly sharp. The old man walked in sandals that he had made from a truck tire; Kitafe wore his sneakers from home, but he would rather have had sandals like his grandfather.

As the day warmed, the fog began to lift and Kitafe was able to see indistinct brown forms moving through a clearing ahead. "Those are impala," the old man told him. "All but one are females; the one with the horns is a buck, a male. He tries to chase all the other bucks away from his ladies."

Kitafe laughed when Morgan called them ladies.

"They are eating the new grass that comes up right after the fires. The old dry grass burns every year and that brings the sweet new grass. If lightening doesn't start the fires, the natives, the rangers and the hunters do. Tall, dead grass can hide dangers like lions, snakes, even buffalo. When it gets dry and tough, the cows and even the goats don't like it. So, it burns."

As they got closer to the clearing, Kitafe could see other, smaller animals amongst the impala. Morgan told him they were warthogs, and they were eating the same new grass. The warthogs took a more direct approach and were eating from down on their knees.

A troop of baboons was also there, big ones, medium sized ones and quite a few tiny ones. The smallest ones rode on their mothers' backs, upright, like little cowboys. The older baboons were picking up something off the ground, which they examined carefully before putting it in their mouths or throwing it away. Alone, high on a tall dead tree, was a fearsome, big old male who Morgan said was the lookout, the "watchdog." "I often see these three animals together in open grassy areas. The baboon is not casual about his watchdog duties; from his high seat, he can look down through the trees and bushes. The impalas are always nervous and alert because all the predators – lions, leopards, wild dogs, hyenas – think they are delicious. I can understand how the baboon and impala sort of work together and benefit each other; more eyes and ears, ever on the alert. I don't know what the warthog brings to this party. Maybe the baboons and impala think that if they are attacked, the warthog will be the easiest one to catch, or maybe they are simply uninvited guests who show up often and stay."

As they approached along the trail, the lookout baboon was looking away and saw something else. His booming, coughing roars sent all the other baboons up the nearest trees. The impalas responded with their own raspy, warning calls and raced off through the surrounding forest. With their tails straight up in the air like little flagpoles, the warthogs galloped away on their short little legs and disappeared into an aardvark hole at the base of a tall termite mound. The clearing was emptied in seconds. The lookout baboon had seen a leopard.

"You will hear those warning calls again Kitafe, usually warning that a predator is afoot. Some of the birds and monkeys also have alert or alarm calls. Often, if a leopard, for instance, is hunting, you can track his progress by the succession of animal and bird alert calls. Trust them; there will not be many false alarms. If you are alert to what they are saying, the birds and animals will tell you a lot about what is happening in the brush and in the forest."

Kitafe didn't say anything, but his mind was reeling from all he was seeing, hearing, learning. Now he began to understand why his parents had sent him to live with the old man. But Morgan was puzzled; he didn't think that he and the boy had spooked the animals in the distant clearing. Maybe a leopard. Maybe not.

Even though they were still a long distance from the big river, Morgan began pointing out the works of the elephants. The effects of a herd of animals, each one eating 600 pounds of forage a day is hard to conceal. The elephants had pushed over many trees, so they could reach the tender top leaves and branches. Other trees had great vertical strips of bark peeled away. Even the enormous baobab trees would often be ringed completely around; the fibrous "bark" supplied the big beasts with moisture in the dry times. The older bulls in particular seemed to push over smaller trees just for the fun of it. Their huge, round footprints dotted the sunbaked mud on the trail. The old man pointed out the divots where they had pulled out clumps of grass and the loose dirt that they had shaken off the roots. It was all so evident to Kitafe when it was explained, but on his own, he would not have noticed.

That first evening they camped beneath the tall trees over-looking a small, clear waterhole. The water was clear, the old man said, because the elephants had not used it all day. They watched the little water hole for the hour before dark.

"Why do the animals drink now?" Kitafe wondered.

"It is because that is their habit, and they have been out in the heat all day. It is also because the lions and leopards hunt at night. While it is still light, the antelope and other smaller animals can see their enemies. At night, the cats can see better."

Last to arrive, before it became too dark for the old man and the boy to see was a small herd of elephants, cows and young-sters. "Where are the man elephants?" asked Kitafe. Morgan was pleased that the boy had noticed that there were no mature bulls in the group.

"This is called a breeding herd. It is all cows and calves and young bulls. They are probably all related. A group like this is very capable of protecting the little ones from danger. The big cow at the edge of the water is called the matriarch. She is their trusted leader, and they follow her imperceptible directions and instruc-tions." He went on, "The bulls are not welcome most of the time, so they hang out with their elephant buddies until one of the cow's calls. It is a lot like the men in our village. They come quickly when they are called."

"But they seem very quiet. I don't hear them calling or even talking," Kitafe said.

"Ah," said the old man. "They are talking all the time. We just can't hear it. I will tell you what I was told by one of the hunters. He said all sound travels in waves, through the air or water or the ground, sort of like waves in the ocean. If the waves are close together, the sound is like a siren or a scream. If the waves are far apart, the sound is like a low rumble, like distant thunder or a lion's roar. Elephants talk in a language where the waves are so far apart that people cannot hear much of what they are saying. But that elephant talk travels far. The hunter told me that a cow elephant can communicate with her friends or a boyfriend maybe as much as five miles away."

"Wow," said Kitafe, "no wonder they have such big ears."

"And that is not all their ears do," Morgan said, "by fanning their ears back and forth they are able to cool their whole body."

CHAPTER 6

ELEPHANT WALK

The old matriarch led her small herd away from the now dirty water hole in the Nyeti Pan to a trail that the elephants had used for decades, maybe even centuries. They would not return for many months. She had led her herd on this trail several times before. Although her eyesight was poor, her superb sense of smell melded into her remarkable memory. Her mind held a virtual library of smells. Although she had not followed this trail for nearly a year, the scents lingered and were clear to her. She probably could have followed it with her eyes closed, but, of course, she didn't.

It is August, late in the dry winter. The rains of the African summer, six months earlier, had filled the shallow pans, the only sources of water on the plateau. The matriarch somehow knew that it would be months before the rains again filled the pans.

As the pans slowly dry up, more and more animals of all sorts converge on a diminishing number of water holes. The many hooves and the animal wastes turn the remaining water muddy and foul. Elephants in particular like clean, clear water. For them, it is time to move on. Other animals could and would deal with the remaining water.

The ancient trail along which she led them wove north, over and down the escarpment toward the Zambezi valley, through forests and brush for nearly 100 miles. It was a dangerous journey for the elephants because unless they could find water every day along the way, the young ones could die. Her deep subconscious somehow told the matriarch she could lead them to it. For an elephant, even water has smell, or maybe an essence. Food was a lesser problem. Elephants can eat a great variety of grasses, shrubs, leaves, branches, bark, fruit. Regarding eating, the herd would be fine; regarding water, they unknowingly and totally trusted the keen senses of the matriarch. Each of them was learning valuable lessons from her, lessons that later could mean their survival.

For Bahati, the migrating trail was a grand adventure. He and his slightly older male cousins play whenever the march pauses, pushing and shoving, wrapping their little trunks together and wandering into the bordering scrub forest. They are adventurers and explorers so long as the herd is in sight. Once in a while, the herd will resume the trek while the kids are off exploring. As soon as they realize that the herd is out of sight, they are all squealing and shrieking and running to where the herd had gone. It would never go far without the little ones and they soon catch up and the reunion is as if they'd been lost for months.

So far, the calves have been fortunate; lions will be a serious threat until the calves grow much bigger. They have left the territory of the Nyeti Pan pride, but other even stronger prides may lie ahead.

The matriarch, who is Bahati's grandmother, keeps the group moving ever northward. So far small, shaded wetlands and cool springs, water seeping from fractures in the rocks of the escarpment have sustained them, but the herd often drains the small water sources in a stop. If another herd has preceded them, and drains a remembered spot, the march continues sometimes for hours, until another source is located. As they descend toward the alley of the Zambezi, fewer and fewer of these small wet areas occur.

During the rainy season, the dry river sand that they are following fills with water rushing northward from the granite highland, from the escarpment toward the Zambezi. The river had followed this course for thousands of years, each year depositing a little more sand. The soft, loose sand the elephants shuffle through is actually tens of feet thick and they are walking over a slowly moving river of water flowing underground through the sand toward the Zambezi. In some places this underground river water is only inches or a foot or two below the surface.

CHAPTER 7

BUSH LESSONS

A s they walked, the old man gently kicked the sand and said, "There is no surface water between here and the big river, but we will probably still see elephants feeding in the adjacent forest. They want water every day and will walk long distances for it if necessary."

Kitafe could hardly believe all that he was learning about the elephants, the river, the forest from the old man. It was the kind of learning he craved, the things he really wanted to know. He believed and tried to remember every word the old man said. Today they did not see any elephants and the boy wondered why.

The old man loved the birds, and he knew them all. He could identify most unseen birds by their call; he knew what their nests looked like, he knew what they ate. But he did not have much luck in interesting Kitafe, who was mostly interested in the big animals. As they walked the sand river, through the dry forest, antelope often appeared in the clearings or crossing the sand. The majestic kudu bulls were the boy's favorite, and in this remote, wild area the kudu would often stand for a few minutes before the quiet brown, upright intruders. The old man explained, "The kudu can live here because they get enough water from the plants they eat, but they would rather drink regularly." The old man thought he liked the giraffes best because they were slow moving and seemed to be at peace with themselves, sort of like the old men of his village. Once, when they got quite close, Kitafe could hardly believe how big they were. "They can look in the window of a three-story house and weigh more than ten men," Morgan told him.

That evening after they ate their meals and the dried antelope meat, which the old man called biltong, they sat closer and closer to the little fire as the damp air quickly cooled. Morgan's mopane wood fire did not spark or smoke. He said to Kitafe, "There are hyenas here, so lay very near the fire. If you wake up, put some more wood on the fire."

Kitafe nodded and said, "We have seen some hyenas, but they seem to be afraid of us. Why are you worried?"

"Because," the old man replied, "they act much differently at night. They can see well at night and they seem to know that people cannot. They become much bolder when they sense that they have an advantage. I think you have seen the man in our village who has only one hand. He fell deeply asleep beside his fire after drinking too much beer, and 'Fisi,' the hyena took it off with one powerful bite. I have seen others missing fingers, toes, even parts of their faces from such bites. It always happens at night."

An uneasy Kitafe spent a restless night, and the fire never went out.

To his knowing eye, the signs in the sand told the old tracker many things – who or what had been there, when, what they were doing. Toward the end of the third day, Morgan noticed something only a skilled and experienced hunter would have seen. Along the east bank of the heavily tracked sand river, the sand was untracked, smooth; there were no animal tracks, no leaves. To him, it was obvious that someone walked here, then, with a tree branch tried to sweep away his tracks. *Why would they do that?* he wondered. *Who are they?* Because there were no new tracks or marks on the swept sand Morgan thought that the action was probably quite recent, and whoever did it was probably nearby. His keen senses were on high alert. Later that evening, before they stopped to camp, he caught the faint smell of wood smoke, and something else. Someone was smoking meat. If he had been alone, Morgan would have followed the smoke smell to see whoever it was that did not want to be seen. But with the boy along, it could be dangerous. They were still some distance from the village, so he suspected that there were poachers here, and they could have guns and certainly would have knives. He did not tell the boy what he suspected.

That evening, the old man made camp a few hundred yards off the sand river, behind a low ridge so that the light from their small campfire could not be seen from the river. He talked quietly, and in response, so did the boy. Morgan did not want any surprise evening visitors.

CHAPTER 8

RIVER OF SAND

The instincts and memory of the old matriarch led the small
herd from the head of one of the north-flowing rivers coming
off the rapidly drying plateau. At this time of the year, they were
methodically plodding down a widening dry riverbed of soft sand.
Their tracks mingled with those of other herds who had passed
earlier, most of them heading north toward the life-giving water
in the river. The tracks of impala, kudu, zebras, giraffes, warthogs,
baboons and the many other residents of this valley of tall trees
pockmarked the sand.

Gentle breezes tell the older elephants who is here and who
has recently passed. They know that Sasha's small herd, heading

in the same direction, passed two or three days earlier and that a bull elephant in musth was following them. The familiar scent of the honey hunter is here too, and the elephants recognize it easily; his honey searches take him several times a year up and over the escarpment. Troubling however is the strong, acrid scent of lions; apparently, the resident, territorial pride.

It is easy walking on the smooth sand and the matriarch leads them at a steady pace. Then, ahead of them, the endless smooth sand road is unexpectedly hummocky and disturbed as though something big had been digging in the loose sand. The smell of elephants is strong. Baboons and banded mongooses are scattered across the lumpy sand surface, occasionally disappearing from sight. The matriarch pauses and raises her trunk to assay what is in front of them. The older elephants see this and quickly follow her lead. A light breeze brings them a familiar scent or essence that they know well. It is water! But where is it in this seemingly endless river of dry sand?

The older members have been down the sand rivers on earlier treks, and they remember. The matriarch begins to kick at the loose sand with a big front foot. Soon she has a hole a little over a foot deep and there in her little hole is water, clear, cool, fresh water. With her trunk, she pulls out more sand until she has a round hole about two feet deep with a foot of clear water at the bottom. The older members of the herd have been in dry sand rivers before and quickly follow her lead.

Bahati's little trunk cannot reach the water as he stands over Njeri's hole; it does not occur to him to kneel down to get closer, so he starts squealing. So does one of the other small ones. Njeri soon realizes why he is so unhappy; drinking a bit herself, she fills her trunk and pumps the cool water into his mouth, under his still floppy trunk. She pumps several trunkfuls into 800 pounds of thirsty young elephant; lots spill but the job is soon done. Then, it is a serious refill for Njeri; they will not drink for another day.

In this dry, thirsty country, the buried water in the river sands is the only available water until the next rainy season, still three months away. Most of the forest creatures that need to drink regularly will get their water from the holes that the elephants dig. Even the giraffes drink from the holes after they have paved away the sand to open a larger hole. Predators are also drawn to the river by the concentration of prey animals, and of course, the water. Little grows in the sand river, but dense brushy under-growth flanks the loose sand and provides excellent cover for the hunters.

Led by the old matriarch, the small herd follows the course of the sand river, heading ever northward, toward the Zambezi. Later in the afternoon, the herd has spread out into the neighboring forest on the east side of the sand river to feed on tender leaves, soft twigs and the drying grass, the adults communicating with low rumbles. The three small ones are busily exploring, unmindful of the rest of the herd.

An abrupt shift in the late afternoon breeze suddenly brings with it a new, but familiar scent. It is the smell of danger, ahead, on the east side, their side, of the river. The scent is that of lions, and the scent is strong. The smaller elephants in the scattered herd are in great danger unless the herd can regroup quickly, very quickly. The adult elephants instantly recognize the lion smell and react by trumpeting and crashing directly into the light breeze. It is a deafening racket that would scare off most threats. The lions, however, do not scare off. They see the opportunity to pick off one of the defenseless, small elephants scattered through the dense brush and trees along the river.

When the trumpeting begins, Bahati had been trying to get the other two bigger, older calves to play. He instantly looks for Njeri, but he doesn't know where she is; in fact, he doesn't know where the herd has gone. Then, as even his floppy little trunk picks up the strong lion scent, a powerful, mature lioness charges into the little group of youngsters. The lioness hurls herself onto Bahati's three-year-old friend, slamming him to the ground. The young elephant is much heavier than the attacker and quickly stands up, only to be knocked down again. She sinks long claws into his back and rakes them crosswise, but he is up again, squealing furiously as are the other two calves. Then, two more lionesses join the fray, grabbing at the young elephants and bowling over little Bahati. He squeals frantically as a heavy lioness lies over him preparing for a final, fatal bite.

The bedlam of the scene is increased by orders of magnitude as the adult elephants from the herd arrive, roaring and trumpeting. An angry elephant is a sight and sound to behold. A young elephant is a fairly easy prey for determined lions, but big elephants can be lion killers and the lions know it well. As quickly as the lions attacked, they were gone, leaving behind three terrified youngsters searching for their mothers.

Bahati is more scared than hurt, but it was a close call that he will not forget. He is bruised but his only real wound is a straight slash across the front of his left hindfoot, a scar he will carry for the rest of his life. Njeri quickly finds him, and he spends the rest of the day and most of the next under her massive belly. For now, this is his home. The calf that was attacked first has long slashes in the thick hide of his back, but he too will heal quickly. As he grows, the scars on his back will also grow and make him easily recognizable for the rest of the trek down the river of sand to the Zambezi. The herd now moves as a tight group, which suits the little ones just fine. It was a nasty scare that will leave long memories and an increased hatred of lions.

CHAPTER 9

TRAILING ELEPHANTS

The old man and the boy followed the same sand river toward the Zambezi, only two days after Njeri and Bahati's herd had passed. The signs of the big animals' journey were clear to Morgan and he explained what he saw to the boy. He pointed out the different grasses, leaves and twigs that they ate, and then he showed him the half-digested remains of those things in their droppings. Half smiling, he said, "If they digested their food better, they wouldn't have to eat so much, and lots of trees would be spared."

Farther along he pointed out the drinking holes that the elephants had dug in the sand, and they filled their own gourds with clear, cool water. Kitafe asked if the water in these old holes was good to drink and the old man told him that the buried water was flowing downstream, just much slower than the surface water flowed during the rainy season. The water in the holes is filtered as it flows through the sand. Later, the story recorded in the sand told the old man about the lion attack and the elephant rescue. He noticed the deep straight cut across one of the calves' feet and wondered how it could have occurred out in this river loose sand. He would never know for sure, but as he thought about it, he couldn't think of anything in nature that would make such a cut. Then, he thought about the abundance of antelope and other smaller animals, the swept area in the dry river sand, the smell of smoke and came to the conclusion that the little elephant perhaps stepped into a trapper's snare, the tight wire cutting deeply before breaking and dropping off.

The old man hated snares because they were so indiscriminate; they caught everything. One set on a trail for a scrub hare or a small antelope could snare an elephant's trunk or a lion's foot or any number of unintended victims. As the animal struggled against the wire, it bit deeper and deeper into the flesh. The small animals that the snare was intended for were choked and died quickly. But he had seen an elephant with its trunk so damaged that it couldn't drink and a lioness that was too crippled to hunt or keep up with the pride. He knew that the snares were an efficient way for a poor man to put some meat on his family's table. But he wished there was another way.

The late afternoon sun was warm on their backs as they climbed a low ridge and at last could see the great river in the distance. Many, many large dark shapes appeared in the water and in the grass along the riverbank.

Later, as the old man prepared their meager supper, Kitafe said, "thank you for bringing me to see the elephants. I never knew that there were so many. There are more than I can count."

Morgan laughed and said, "Isn't it wonderful?"

Kitafe was so excited he could hardly sleep. He was up and started their little fire in the dark as the eastern horizon was only beginning to lighten. He used the last of their water from the elephant holes and boiled tea.

When Morgan woke, he sat by the fire, drank his tea, and spoke solemnly to his grandson. "Yesterday, I told you that we must be cautious when we are near the elephants. There are certain situations where the elephants can be extremely dangerous, dangerous to us. For instance, an elephant mother is totally protective of her calf. All his life, she has protected him from anything that might harm him … lions, crocodiles, hyenas, people. Another situation that is potentially dangerous is if we should startle or surprise one; you don't know which of his 'fight' or 'flight' reactions will prevail. So, what I think we should do is to let the elephants know that we are here and are not a threat. We will get upwind of them so they get our scent, we will talk quietly so they hear us, and we will move slowly where they can see us. For our safety and their peace of mind we will not attempt to get close to them."

"Now," he said, "watch the smaller groups. A mature cow will often have several of her own offspring around her. She has a baby about every five years. So, if she has a new baby with her, there will probably be a five-year-old and a ten-year-old brother or sister close by." Soon Kitafe was pointing out the little family groups to his grandfather.

When the sun had risen above the trees and was warm on their back, they walked slowly toward the river. As they stopped beside a termite mound, they were partially hidden from the elephants, hippos and the grazing animals on the grassy flood plain.

All day they watched the same few groups of elephants. They would gather small bunches of one particular grass with their trunks and place it carefully in their mouths. Other times they would grab clumps of another grass that were so large they couldn't stuff it all in their mouth. Some of them appeared to be sleeping standing up. Once a group, including a baby, waded into the river. The big elephants surrounded it, protecting it from the current, but also because they knew that crocodiles could be anywhere in this river. Kitafe noticed that the little one had its mouth up under his mother's front leg. "What is he doing, grandfather?"

"He is nursing," Morgan laughed, "you see a mother elephant's milk is between her front legs, not between the back legs like our cows and goats."

"How old do you think he is?" the boy asked.

"Well look," said the old man, "he still has some of his baby hair, and he can easily walk under his mother's belly, so I think he is less than one year old. When he is about a year old, his baby hair will be gone, and he will probably be too tall to walk under her. He will still be nursing but will have to do it from the side. He will be with her or near her until he is twelve to fifteen years old. Then, he will be encouraged to join other male elephants away from the breeding herd. The females will remain with the herd so that a forty-year-old cow elephant may have several direct offspring in the herd, some with calves of their own. Most of the elephants in the breeding herd are relatives."

CHAPTER 10

VILLAGE LIFE

As he hoed the weeds from his rows of sorghum, Azaan, the honey hunter, could look across his small field to see his wife and the two boys carrying pails of water from the river. They would pour the water into the weeded troughs that Azaan had scraped out between the closely spaced rows of grain. There had not been a drop of rain in nearly five months. The four of them, just like the other families along the river, had carefully tended their modest crops for many hot months and the time to harvest was near. The small sorghum field and a vegetable garden would provide much of their food for the next six months. His wife would later pound the dried grain kernels into a powder, store it in bags and place it in their storage shed along with dried garden vegetables and some smoked meat and fish. The storage shed stood on six-foot-high stilts to protect their food from rising river levels, monkeys and baboons and the small animals and bugs that swarmed the ground at night.

The people of the little village were of the Tonga tribe, a tribe that had lived on the south bank of the Zambezi for many generations. Life had changed little in those years with one great exception: the villages were no longer raided by the Arab slave traders.

It is a hard life in the little villages along the river. Many children die of disease, crops fail, torrential storms destroy shelters, elephants and baboons can raid, even destroy the only crops. Lions and leopards are a constant threat to goats and the few cows.

Every day Azaan's wife would make "mealie meal," a thick porridge made form sorghum flour. She would add vegetables from the garden or fish that Azaan had speared and occasionally some meat from an animal he had caught in his wire snares. All fifteen of the families in this village lived in similar mud and reed huts, cultivated sorghum, millet and small vegetable patches and ate mainly mealie meal. If Azaan brought back honey or wild fruits from his long treks to the escarpment, he would share, and the bland mealie meal became much tastier.

CHAPTER 11

YAZID

Yazid Mulanga was born and raised in a small village of farmers on the north bank of the Zambezi River. He was his mother's first and only child. She died of malaria and complications related to his birth before his first birthday. He was raised by a willing grandmother with occasional, but undependable, help from his father.

Yazid's father did a bit of farming, but trading was his preferred livelihood. In his old, battered, aluminum John-boat with a smoking, sputtering 25-horse engine, he moved mainly farm products between villages. Occasionally, once or twice a year, a large cargo barge from far downriver would bring rarely seen items, which Yazid's father would purchase, store and later resell or trade to the river villagers. The cargo vessel also brought a large drum of gasoline for the little outboard motor. There were no other motorboats on this section of the river.

Everyone seemed to like the trader, a big happy fellow who loved to talk. He carried the news and gossip between widely separated villages. He was even the occasional matchmaker alerting the young and not so young of possible available mates. About the time Yazid was fourteen years old, his father broke his right forearm. One of the midwives in the village tried to set the broken bone, but it never fused straight or solidly and pained the big man for the rest of his life.

Thus, began Yazid's life on the river. His father needed help and quite a bit of it. He had, for instance, trouble lifting or turning things. He could steer the boat, but had trouble pulling the cord to start the motor. Yazid seemed to inherit his father's cheery, happy personality, and he liked the trading, and being on the river and he was especially happy with the village girls he met. When he was twenty-three years old, his father suddenly died, and Yazid took over the little river trading business whose tangible assets were the battered John-boat and a heavy old dugout canoe that his father had inherited from his father. The dugout was rarely put in the water but was kept for use when the gasoline barrel was empty. The older trader also used it as a bargaining ploy if he was trying to convince someone that he was himself desperately poor.

Yazid was as good a trader as his father had been, but with the limited resources the region offered, it was difficult for him to build his business in a significant, consistent way. For many men living along the river, their goal in life was simply comfortable subsistence. Yazid knew that he wanted something different. He had unclear ambitions, but he knew he wanted to build something and see it grow. And he desperately wanted a better boat and motor.

Several years after his father died, Yazid met the big cargo barge on its annual upstream trading mission. He would buy the things that the village farers forgot to buy or didn't need at the time. He always bought a lot of cured tobacco because he knew the farmers always ran out and would tire of the harsh tobacco they grew in their gardens. Coffee was a luxury, but seldom drunk except on special occasions because of its cost. Yazid always had some available. He would also buy the cheap costume jewelry, which he knew a courting young gentleman would absolutely have to have and price would be no object. He was a clever, but bored trader.

As Yazid finished loading his purchases from the big trading boat into the flat-bottomed John-boat, a slim, light complexioned man approached and offered a cigarette and a light. He asked quietly about Yazid's trading business, particularly about what sort of products he traded for, what was available, what made him the most money. He was also curious about the legality of different trade items and whether any sort of law enforcement was present on this section of the river. The stranger told Yazid that he too was a trader and part owner of the very boat they were standing on. He came from a city far downstream in Mozambique and he had buyers there who would pay very well for fish and bushmeat. Did Yazid think any of the river villagers would be interested in supplying these? "Check around," he said, "if they are, we can discuss details when the boat returns back down the river in a month or so."

Yazid, the enterprising trader, quickly saw that if he could put himself between the sellers of these products and the rich buyer, there was some serious money to be made. He needed a plan and he needed it soon, so he could discuss a deal with the pale man when his cargo barge came back.

Yazid didn't know much about bushmeat animals and the bushmeat trade, other than that many native people still craved it after moving into the cities. From the hushed conversation he had just had, he suspected that the trade was probably illegal. The village people living along the river routinely trapped and snared a few animals for the pot, but there was little organized trading and selling.

The young trader had plenty of time to think as his old boat puttered up or down the river. His gas supply was never secure enough for him to travel very far from his home village, but he thought of villages and people he hadn't met before. He thought of the areas with perhaps more game or better fishing. If this bushmeat business was illegal, he thought, he certainly did not want his home villagers to know that he was involved.

Yazid was a more-than-capable riverman, but he was not a hunter, trapper or a man skilled in the bush; however, he had a good friend who was. Rafiki was an age group brother who strived to support a new young wife and a rapidly approaching baby. He was known in the village as a successful hunter, trapper and fisherman, but a lazy, derelict farmer.

Rafiki was delighted with an opportunity to get far away from the tedious, unending work of crops and goats. The plan he and Yazid came up with could end his farm work forever. Their strategy was to locate an area with good game populations, river and land trail access, and a poor, nearby village to provide hunters.

Two days after their first conversation, the two men loaded the old John-boat with some basic supplies and all the gas that Yazid thought he could risk, and they headed upstream to scout for a place that fit their simple requirements. They ran slowly upriver against a strong current, hugging the southern bank, for all of that day and most of the next until distant smoke from a riverside village came drifting to them. Some two miles downstream of where they thought the smoke originated, they pulled ashore on the south side of the big river and into the mouth of a rapidly drying tributary. They wanted to keep their scouting mission hidden from any locals at this time. A cool, heavy fog descended on them as they sat in the boat and ate a cold meal of mealies and biltong.

As they sat cold and wet the next morning, waiting for the fog to lift, Rafiki pointed to a man passing in the early light. He seemed to be carrying a number of wire snares in his left hand. "Let us follow him; he probably knows the forest trails. He has not seen us. He can be our unpaid guide to this area where we have been seeing good numbers of antelope." They followed the wandering trail of the trapper as quietly as possible for several hours until Yazid halted and proclaimed, "We are now so far from the river that getting meat from larger animals back to the boat would be difficult and we could risk spoilage. He does not seem to have come from the village that we could smell. Let us carefully scout this area back to the river, and perhaps follow him again. Then, let us visit the village."

Six weeks later, when the trading barge came back down the river, Yazid and Rafiki were waiting by the village where Yazid had first spoken with the pale man who wanted to buy bushmeat. They had spent many days upstream in the forest checking game varieties, animal numbers, the game trail network. The game trails were well-used, and the men envisioned sites where traps or snares could be set. An added benefit of the area was that it was an unleased communal area lying between a national park and a safari area leased by the government to a professional hunter. Hippos grazed the area close to the river, and they could be dangerous, but they did not see lions at this time.

When Yazid and Rafiki presented their three-part plan to the pale trader, they couldn't tell if he was pleased or disappointed; the face of the trader showed no emotion. They only knew that he approved when he told them that the next thing to do should be a visit to the nearby village to gauge what sort of interest there was in joining the bushmeat trade.

When Yazid mentioned that they had seen a lone trapper a few weeks earlier, the pale man surprised them saying, "I have a few trappers scattered along the river, but they harvest only a few animals. They trap by themselves and do not work very hard; money hardly seems to motivate them. I have built a river camp to process larger numbers of animals than these few lone trappers can supply. I would like to have more hunters, reliable hunters, a more organized an efficient operation. Your idea to get a number of trappers from a single village would meet my needs very well. Because of my appearance and culture, I cannot effectively recruit among these people. Sometimes in business there is need for a middleman between the buyer and the seller. I think you could be that person."

"Meet me at my camp, several miles upriver from here. You will see a yellow flag on the north bank. The camp is up a small tributary, behind tall reeds on the opposite bank."

CHAPTER 12

LIONS COME

In the warm afternoon sun, both the old man and the boy fell asleep in the soft grass for a long time. Morgan heard it first: Uuung! Uuung! Uuung! Kitafe woke a minute later. Soon the sound was closer and louder, much louder. All the animals along the river, except the hippos, seemed more alert, nervous and wary, looking in the direction of the sounds. "A pride of lions approaches," said the old man. Kitafe was worried about the other animals, especially the little elephants. But the old man said, "They are safe. The lions come only to drink. They will do their hunting at night."

The elephants seemed to know this too. But the little ones still hurried to their mothers, the smallest, under their mama. The big cows trumpeted loudly, telling the lions not to come any closer and they did not come a step closer.

The lions drank slowly and deeply, then quietly padded back into the brush, the cubs frolicking and tumbling and chasing the butterflies and birds. They too knew that their mamas would protect them.

Grandfather and grandson returned to their little camp on the hill for one last night before heading into the village and Azaan's place. This night, as Morgan was building a much larger fire he said, "the lions do not like fire and although I like lions at a distance, I do not like them in camp at night." Kitafe lay as close to the fire as he could without burning himself, but he again did not sleep well.

The next morning the lions were calling a couple of miles upriver, to the west. And then, they were heard no more. When Kitafe and Morgan returned to their lookout place by the termite mound, they quickly saw that a new visitor had arrived. It was a different elephant, a great bull elephant with long, dirty tusks. He was much bigger, much taller than any of the others. He was fully twelve feet high at the top of his shoulder.

The other elephants in Njeri's little herd ignored him or walked away with their calves. Some of the older cows probably knew him, but they did not seem to want him here. And the bull knew they did not want him with them. He was muttering to himself as he marched off. "He is going back to be with the boys," the old man said.

"Tomorrow we will go down to the small river village, the one you can see upstream, this side of tall trees and across from the white sand bar. We will stay with Azaan and his family. He is my son and your uncle." Kitafe was anxious to meet relatives he had never seen before. The thought of a woman's cooking sounded especially good. Morgan was not a very good cook for a young boy's tastes.

CHAPTER 13

THE RIVER

A gentle, soft wave of excitement had been coursing through the matriarch's herd during the morning. Towering apple-ring acacia trees, with great spreading branches, formed a shady canopy over the lower reaches of the sand river. The last of the seed pods were falling. The pods are small and flat, but the elephants seemed to love them above nearly all else. Ponderously, they would shuffle after every newly fallen pod. Shortly, there are none left on the ground, but the big animals would patiently wait for another to fall. Weeks earlier, before the elephants arrived, Azaan's wife, Anoona, had gathered large bags of the same pods;

she would later pound the dark brown seeds to make a nutritious flour and a better tasting mealie meal.

Picking up seed pods slowed the little herd's progress, but as the tall trees along the dry sand river merged with the wall of Acacia trees on the banks of the Zambezi and the sand river ran into the bordering high grass and reeds, the matriarch knew that she had done it again. But she had never doubted. Elephants don't doubt!

In front of them, in the smooth flowing water, only the eyes and nostrils of a herd of hippos broke the surface. Two weathered old crocodiles had hauled up, half out of the water, onto a white island sandbar. Two old "dagga boy" buffalo bulls were half sunken in the warm mud of a little cut-out across the river.

It is as she remembered, a place alive with the sounds of birds, the snorting of hippos, and the soft rustle of the breeze in the tall trees. There were interesting smells on the breeze, which for Bahati were new, but the matriarch recognized and remembered them from previous journeys. There was wood smoke from Azaan's village, four miles upstream, the sweet scent of the ripening sorghum, lilies and the flowering marsh grasses in the back channels, and the rank smell of a nearby waterbuck. In minutes the dry, dusty herd was drinking cool clear water. To the north, looming over the lush green valley of the Zambezi, is the towering Zambian Escarpment, an arm of the East African Rift System. Bleak, dark and foreboding, it is not welcoming to man or beast. Few animal trails and no roads cross it here.

The matriarch cautiously led her group into a shallow side channel, searching for and finding a firm sandy bottom. Bahati hadn't been in the water since getting stuck in the mud at Nyeti

Pan some months ago, and he approached timidly as did Njeri with her own vivid memories. Soon the entire herd was in the water, drinking, spraying, some even submerging completely. A couple of the big younger elephants were happily playing with each other in the deeper water of the main river. Bahati stayed close to his mother as she slowly waded in, aware that her little son's last water experience had been terrifying for both of them. Here, however, the sand bottom was firm, almost hard and the small one's confidence returned quickly.

The cool river water soothed their bodies and senses and a sort of calm settled over them, seeming to wash away memories of the month-long trek from the dry plateau far to the south.

Soon Bahati was splashing and pushing around his little elephant friends in the shallower parts of the river. He wanted to spray water out of his trunk like the big ones did, but he still hadn't mastered his little trunk; spraying would have to wait. Older members of the herd went into the deeper water. Sometimes only the tips of a trunk would tell that a submerged elephant was there. Some of them seemed to be splashing for no reason other than the sheer joy of it. It was a happy herd of elephants that afternoon.

But the matriarch was wary as always. She knew that the big crocs would attack a young calf given an opportunity. Today the crocs were given no opportunity. After more than an hour in the water, the elephants slowly returned to the shade of the tall trees. Bahati was still nursing, so he was a most hungry and tired little elephant as he trundled out of the river beside Njeri.

In the early morning, several hundred yards upstream from the drowsy elephants was a pair of African fish eagles. They scarcely seemed to move from their perch on a dead branch near the top of a tall acacia tree. Both peered through the fog rising off the river, waiting until they could use their extraordinary eyesight to hunt. Even from this height, they could see the tiny disturbances on the water surface created by the small fish feeding below.

It also allowed them to see a rust-colored goliath heron, searching for fish among the reeds, nearly half a mile away. The eagles considered him a poacher on the river. Although the heron was four feet tall, the eagles attacked as soon as they saw him. Both of them were shrieking continuously as they dived on the big bird, often passing within a foot of his head and long neck. Although they did not strike him, their "Go Away" message was very clear. He was a slow, clumsy flier and if he got into the air, the eagles could and probably would kill him. Instead, the tall bird disappeared into the nearby reeds, which towered three feet above his head. The eagles really did not want to kill the heron, but they could not tolerate another fisherman on their river, especially as good a fisherman as a Goliath Heron.

The sudden shrieking cries of the eagles startled and alarmed the elephants whose instinctive reaction to being frightened was flight or fight. Bahati was terrified and reacted instantly by fleeing under Njeri. The adults were too mystified to react at all as the disturbance ended as suddenly as it had begun.

CHAPTER 14

VILLAGE VISITORS

Several gaunt, surly dogs growled from their stations in the dirt as the old man led Kitafe slowly through the little village. Morgan's smooth, low voice seemed to convince the dogs that these intruders were not a threat. Azaan's small house and garden were reached by a wide path between the little buildings. It was a foot and bicycle path. There were no vehicles in the village; boats and the river were the only access to and from the outside world.

As they walked into Azaan's fenced yard through some scrawny chickens, Morgan was a bit surprised that no dog met them. His son had always had a dog or two since he was a little boy. Azaan was working in the garden when he saw his father and the boy come through the fence. "I see you, honored father" he called. And heard back, "I see you, my son." They were both smiling; it had been more than a year since they had been together. Their talk brought out Anoona from inside and she too was most happy to see the old gentleman and his young friend who she had not met before. "My boys were supposed to be helping me in the garden, but they sort of vanished; I am sure they are playing along the river. They really aren't much help anyway."

There were two log benches around a rocked-in fire pit and the four of them chatted there about family things, village things, crops and, of course, the weather. Kitafe's father was Azaan's brother; so, the boy told him about their life in the city … the cars, the stores, the schools, the soccer team. Then, a little glance from Morgan, and he knew he'd talked enough. Morgan had run out of pipe tobacco and he asked Azaan if he had some. He did but it was the harsh, big-leafed uncured tobacco that he grew in his garden. After the men had filled and lit their pipes, the old man asked why Azaan had no dogs; he would have needed them to protect the chickens and the garden from raiders like monkeys and baboons and mongooses and leopards. Azaan explained that three nights before, a leopard went after the chickens and the dog tried to protect them and was killed. Often, the barking of a dog will chase a leopard away. But few dogs are a match for a hungry determined leopard. "I will have to get another one to be a guard here, but I also like to have a dog along when I go for the honey; they are good company. And I wanted to tell you that I think I have had the same little, chirping honey guide for the last few trips."

Morgan and his wife had lived in the little riverside village for most of their lives but left a few years earlier when the old lady had health issues and it was unsafe for her to be in a place as remote as this, so many hours from any medical help. The old man asked about his old friends that he remembered from when they had lived here and was pleased to hear that they were mostly still here, doing what they'd always done with help from now bigger, stronger kids. Azaan was the only honey hunter, the only one that regularly went deep into the forest.

The old man knew the surrounding bush and forest well, from his years of tracking for the professional hunter and wondered where Azaan had recently been trekking. He told his father about the last trip, where two young elephants had killed a hyena and the beehive and the rickety ladder that he'd left in the bushes. But then he said, "Father, this seems most unusual, but I believe that I was not alone. I did not see anyone, but I twice heard sounds that I don't think were made by animals and I heard the go-away birds' alarm call behind me. No one from the village would be that far out in the forest. I think whoever was there did not want me to know he was there."

"That is most interesting" the old man replied. "We too saw signs of someone who did not want to be seen, and we smelled the smoke from a meat-smoking fire. I wondered that, if they were simply natives traveling through the country, why would they try to hide form us?" Morgan said, "Tell me this, do you see a lot of game animals, especially antelope? And elephants; I think that we traveled down one of their traditional dry season routes to the river."

"You are right, father, large numbers of elephants come down that valley every year in the dry season. The area has not been hunted for years. It is a travel route for the elephants, but the antelopes live there year-round. There are many of them, especially impala, but also the big antelope: kudu, sable and eland."

The old man paused, looked off into the distance, relit his pipe and asked, "Azaan, have any strangers come through here or maybe on the river?"

"Not near the village" Azaan answered, "but one of our men just returned from visiting relatives far down the river and, as he was returning, he saw a boat he had not seen before. It had a long canvas tent covering that came down nearly to the gunnels so he could not see who or what was on board. It had a single large outboard motor mounted on the stern. There was a fire burning on shore and he heard voices. He did not know if the boat people saw him as he passed on the far side of the river. Of course, the big trading boat made its annual run up the river, but it does not stop here."

"But now," said Azaan, "as I think about it, a couple of months ago, two men, strangers, arrived from downstream in an old metal boat with a smoking motor. They had few belongings with them, and we wondered where they were coming from. They stayed for two days and left back downstream the way they had come."

"Did you speak with them?"

"Yes, they talked with nearly everybody, asking about the forest animals, the abundance of fish and especially about the elephants, and they wondered what we needed or wanted. They spoke a different dialect of our language, but we could understand them, and they could understand us. They had a lot of tobacco, which they shared, and everyone seemed to like them. But we all wondered what they were doing here and where they had come from."

"I believe you will see them again," said the old man. "I don't think that their coming to your village the first time was an accident. They probably want something that you or the villagers can provide. The next time government game rangers come by, I think you should mention these men and the unfamiliar boat."

CHAPTER 15

NEW COMPANY

After the two troublesome young bulls had been forced out of the matriarch's herd, they wandered around the familiar ground for several days, eating what they had been eating, drinking where they had been drinking. But the branches, leaves and grasses were getting drier and tougher, and the water holes were warm and foul. And they missed the companionship of other elephants. They had to move, and they instinctively moved north toward the great river, along a route they had followed with their mothers and the matriarch many times.

The smell of other elephants, bull elephants, was in the air, always ahead of them as they trudged northward. On the second day, the young bulls, now fifteen years old, and as big as their mothers, heard the breaking of branches and the low rumbling of other elephants ahead of them. Although the young bulls could not see them through the thick brush, they hurried forward. Then, immediately in front of them were four of their own kind; two huge bulls, forty or forty-five years old, a smaller bull of maybe thirty years, and a younger one, probably only a few years older than them. Trunks extended they all tested the air for a couple of minutes without moving. Then, the big ones resumed eating. The young bulls had been accepted, not welcomed but tolerated. This was to be their new family.

It was to be a different life than living win the matriarch's big social family. There was little affection or hostility among the bulls. The strong and necessary leadership of the matriarch was not required here. The two young bulls were awed by the sheer size of the old bulls and they attempted to do as they did, where they did, when they did. Above all else, they did not want to anger or irritate their huge new companions.

At this time of the year, one of the older bulls' chosen foods were the leaves, branches and bark of the acacia trees. A popular elephant pastime seemed to be pushing over these trees, especially the knob thorn acacias. They destroyed the bigger trees by rocking them more and more violently until eventually the tree would snap. Smaller trees would simply succumb to a heavy push from the massive animal's head. Other times the elephants would use a tusk to pry loose a strip of bark, then grabbing the bark with their trunk, they could rip off a long strip of bark that only broke off when it reached a high branch. The bulls would chew the bark, but often left downed trees after eating only a miniscule amount of the leaves and twigs. Sometimes they would eat none at all after working relentlessly to push over a particularly strong tree. The young bulls only watched but pushing over trees probably looked to them like it could be fun. As the little group trekked north-ward toward the Zambezi Valley, they passed through large areas of mopane scrub, areas that had once been an open forest of large mopane trees. It, of course, did not occur to them that generations of elephants had created the scrub forest.

New smells, old smells, remembered smells filled the young bulls' trunks as they descended to the river. Although the old bulls were far larger than anything else in the valley, they were wary and curious. Each tested the air through a raised trunk and listened patiently through huge, extended ears. The young ones copied the old bulls and tried to sort out what the smells and noises were telling them. The elephants' sense of smell, far more refined than any dog's, told them the most. They trusted this sense far more than what their myopic eyes could show them and although the elephant's hearing is acute, the news it brings is only one-dimensional.

All senses operating, they immediately identified a pod of hippos in the river, another small group of elephants downstream, lush river grasses, clear cool water, and the apple ring pods of the acacia. Scents from upriver, however, concerned the older ones. It was cook smoke and other smells they associated with man, a possible threat to the group. The oldest bull had carried an old muzzle-loader rifle slug, lodged near the base of his left tusk for nearly twenty years. The surface wound eventually healed, but the lead slug pressed on a nerve and caused him nearly constant pain. He could not use that tusk for peeling bark from trees or digging in the mineral-rich earth, which elephants crave. The other old bull was also wary of the man smell; he too had been shot while raiding a native garden. His wounds were surficial as the home-made muzzle-loader had only been loaded with small pebbles and scraps of rusty metal. The shot hurt and the loud noise was frightening. Both of them remembered the incidents well. The man smell was interesting to the young elephants, but it did not carry a danger warning message to them.

CHAPTER 16

TEMPTATION

The two men paddling and poling upstream in a shiny aluminum canoe carefully avoided the many pods of partially submerged hippos. The huge territorial hippos bull with each pod was extremely dangerous to anyone or anything that the old bull thought had entered into his space. It was nearing the end of the dry season and animals of all kinds were near the water. Many small breeding herds of elephants caught the men's particular attention; they knew that the bull elephants were probably not too far away.

The villagers remembered the two men and the tobacco they brought and were glad to see them. Visitors of any kind were seldom seen, and they brought news of the outside world.

This time, after the friendly formalities and small talk, the visitors were direct about the reason for their second visit to the village. They were traders or buyers and they wanted to buy game and fish for a downriver city in Mozambique. They could buy or trade. They would provide the wire for snares, salt for curing meat and hides, perhaps even guns and bullets. And tobacco and alcohol. They could change how the villagers lived. Things could be much better.

The men said that they had visited other villages downriver since there was a large demand for meat in the growing city. Lax game laws and corrupt authorities in parts of Mozambique had resulted in severe depletion of the local fish and game resources. The two men suspected that strict national game laws were in effect along this part of the river, but the area is remote, and the laws are seldom violated. In reality, the villagers' subsistence lifestyle required them to take little. There was no significant commercial trade. A visit from one of the State Game Rangers was nearly always more of a social visit than any sort of an enforcement action. But there were laws, and the rangers would enforce them for obvious violations. The villagers were discrete, they did not take much, and the rangers did not search very hard for minor violations.

Azaan, acting as a spokesman for the village, told the two men to return a few days later, after the villagers had discussed the proposal and the two boatmen slowly left after passing out bags of cured tobacco. Azaan was most pleased that his father was in the village at the time to help him deal with this completely unexpected situation.

The old man began the conversation by saying, "Azaan, I do not trust these men. We know nothing about them, and they are asking you to approve something illegal. The trapping and snaring is something that some in the village are already doing, but on an extremely limited scale. Subsistence poaching is a totally different activity than large scale commercial poaching. The rangers will overlook a few snares or traps set to feed a man's family, but they will harshly pursue and prosecute commercial poachers. You could, perhaps, get some legal benefit from selling these men some fish. The big Vundu Catfish are abundant and easy to catch and I am not aware of any protective regulations on them. They can weigh twenty or even thirty kilos; they are as heavy as the small antelope."

The next day, when Azaan and Morgan discussed the proposal with the villagers, the responses varied; it would be good to have some of the things that the money could buy, but they were mostly things the older folks never had or thought they needed. Some of the younger people could think of things that they would like if they had money. Two of the young men, single men with no families, said they would like to get into it. One of them wanted money for a dowry; the other wanted to buy a power boat. When the old man explained that they had good relations with the rangers because they weren't violating the game laws, but that the relation would quickly change if they joined the poachers. Convictions meant jail time for individuals in the nastiest of African jails. He told them of his idea of selling the big catfish. He did not think it was his place to tell anyone what he thought they should do individually.

CHAPTER 17

CHIKU AND HUTO

The little group of bull elephants was about two miles upriver from the matriarch, Njeri, Bahati and the rest of the family but they were only vaguely aware of each other. One of the younger cows in the breeding herd, Chiku, was, after suckling her calf for more than two years, finally free of her progressively bigger, rougher son who had now begun to grow sharp little tusks. He would stay with her and the herd for years, but he would not be constantly bothering her. He could feed himself just fine. She felt free at last.

One morning, after the matriarch's herd had been at the river for about a week, Chiku did something quite strange. She planted her feet firmly and began to rumble loudly. The herd rumbled among themselves constantly; it was their language and the way they communicated. It was a language that only elephants understand. This morning, however, Chiku's rumbling seemed somehow different, and it was. Cow elephants spend most of their adult life either pregnant or nursing, about twenty-two months pregnant and roughly two years nursing their young.

Chiku liked the process and now, without a nursing calf, her rumbling was telling bull elephants in the area that she wanted to be a mother again. Her great flat, spongy feet transmitted her rumblings into firm ground like low frequency seismic waves. Upstream, the old bulls received a somewhat unclear message. They would consider it in the slow deliberate way of elephants.

In the days that followed, the dominant bull, Huto, began to change. He was progressively less tolerant of the behavior of the two young bulls; he was even grouchy with his old friends of many years. The temporal glands on each side of his face swelled and began to seep a dark liquid that eventually reached the corner of his mouth. He dribbled constantly and smelled terrible; it was his message to a receptive cow that he was ready, more than willing and all together able. He was so irritable that all the other bulls in the little group tried to keep away from him.

Downriver, Chiku was also sending scent messages to whoever was interested. Eventually a strong east breeze, coming up the Zambezi Valley, carried her message to Huto and he was quickly on his way. She did not know him, but was glad to see him, a huge elephant, nearly twelve feet tall with long heavy tusks. She wanted no lesser bull to be the father of her baby. He was enormous, smelly, and scary and the herd drifted away. Only Chiku waited anxiously, and the bull of her dreams came to her.

Elephants are extremely fertile, and she conceived easily. When Huto moved away, the herd gathered around and seemed to celebrate the event with contented rumbling. Bahati had no idea what had happened or what they seemed to be celebrating. He would learn. He had a lot to learn.

Huto was agitated and irritable. He did not want to return to the company of the little band of bulls or stay with the matriarchs where he was clearly no longer welcome. So, he wandered east, hoping to find other welcoming cow elephants. Abruptly, a few days later, he realized that he wasn't alone; another big bull, a stranger to Huto, was on a similar quest. Huto hadn't seen him yet but he smelled as bad as Huto and his presence was obvious. A day later they met in a grassy clearing under tall, apple ring acacia trees; the stranger was picking up the few remaining seed pods when Huto entered the clearing from the forest shadows. For long moments, the two grouchy giants glared at each other. Only the hum of insects broke the silence.

Suddenly, the stranger bellowed a trumpeting battle cry, and six tons of screeching fury crashed into Huto. Huto caught the full impact on his trunk, avoiding the deadly incoming tusks. He had fought other elephants and he was able to avoid the tusks, which he knew could kill him if he exposed a flank. Huto was taller and heavier, and he absorbed the impact and pushed the stranger backward, to the edge of the clearing. Huto backed off from their now intertwined tusks and trunks and was promptly charged again, but this time it was with less force or enthusiasm. The clash of the giants was quickly over. As the stranger disengaged, turned and retreated into the forest, Huto followed and casually attempted to drive his tusks into the departing end of his new enemy. In a month, they could probably be friends.

Huto was agitated and surly and would remain in the musth condition for weeks, a threat and danger to all he encountered. He would only return to his little bachelor herd some weeks later, tired, thin, and not nearly so grouchy. He would be ready for some peace and quiet and the company of friends.

CHAPTER 18

THE VISIT

As Rafiki and Yazid paddled upriver toward Azaan's village, they now began to see a number of bull elephants roaming around the breeding herds of cows and calves. Huto and others carried impressive ivory, 60 to 80 pounds and more per tusk. As the dry season progressed, more and more antelopes were drawn to the river flood plain, where they mingled freely and unafraid among forest giants. Rafiki, a short, thick man with a missing front tooth, smiled and said, "This looks better than I had hoped," and then added, "but we need to be patient. The old man does not like us or trust us. His son is sort of the village headman." Yazid, a slender quiet man, agreed. He too felt Morgan's scrutiny and hostility.

When they reached the village and climbed the bank to hear what the village had decided about their offer, Azaan led them to the log bench seats around the ever-burning fire. "The villagers can do as they wish," he said, "and deal with you individually. My father and I have recommended to them that we sell only fish to you. We can, at this time, deliver you eleven Vundu Catfish, which weigh about eighteen kilos each. You would need to send your larger boat up here to pick them up."

"There is no red meat?" asked Rafiki.

"Not that I know of," said Azaan, "but I know you have been trying to deal with individual villagers. I must tell you that I have told the wildlife rangers of your proposal."

The two men left early the next morning in Yazid's old aluminum John-boat and that same afternoon, a large power boat appeared to pick up the catfish. It then stopped a mile or so downstream, out of sight of the village, to onload several heavy bags.

CHAPTER 19

GARDEN RAIDERS

During the time that Huto was traveling, the little bachelor herd remained along the south riverbank eating the riverine grasses and an assortment of other palatable plants. Occasionally, they would catch the sweet smell of maize and sorghum drifting downriver from the gardens in Azaan's village. The older bulls knew well that the village crops could come at a terrible price, and although seriously attracted, they resisted the temptation.

The two young bulls had no experience with men, except the honey hunter who passed quietly through the forest and did not frighten them at all. One evening, without the not-so-subtle guidance of Huto, the bachelor herd was scattered beneath the tall trees south of the river feeding on some tough, but tasty dry grass. They were less than a mile from Azaan's village, as the two young friends drifted toward the village of a dozen huts, surrounded by small plots of vegetables, melons, maize, and sorghum. As it grew dark, fires burned down, and the village grew quiet. Only a couple of skinny dogs were still somewhat awake. The young bulls first sampled the sorghum farthest from the huts. It was delicious, the best food they had ever eaten. The noise of their initially cautious feeding gradually grew louder. The keen ears of the dogs heard them; soon every dog in the village was barking ferociously. Shouting men, banging pans, and carrying torches were running hard toward the precious crops. The terrified young elephants fled down river in total panic. The old bulls knew instantly that the young bulls had been in the village gardens and drifted away in disapproval.

Two nights later, the two returned to the fields again. The last visit was scary, but they hadn't been hurt. They waited until a cloud covered the moon and the night was dark and silent. The smells from individual crops guided them on this darkest of nights. They fed quietly for half an hour, their great flat feet crushing far more than they ate. Then, one of the huge feet crushed a dried melon and the dogs heard it. Almost instantly the still night was filled with noise and movement: racing dogs, shouting men, torches, and a new loud booming noise. Metal scraps, small stones, broken glass from the village's three muzzle loaders rocked the two very surprised elephants. Again, the frightened elephants fled downriver into the forest. Only the shots hitting them in the face penetrated the skin, and none hit their eyes. They returned to the now wary herd, a bit damaged but intact.

After four days of drying grass, bark and limbs, the young bulls returned again to the sweet moist Sorghum. The old matriarch may have been able to dissuade the youngsters from the night raids, but the older bulls simply turned and moved away. Maybe they sensed that tonight was somehow to be different. A steady breeze blew up the river from the elephants toward the village, making it impossible for the young raiders to assess the current situation, conditions, or activity around the garden plots. It was perfectly quiet and dark throughout the twelve huts, nothing moved, the dogs were quiet. The two stood cautiously at the edge of the field of tall sorghum. The heavy grain heads on each stalk were hard, brown, and nearly ready to be harvested. But it was the moist sugary stalks that so attracted the elephants. The night was totally quiet, and the persistent breeze was still from behind them. Tonight, their acute senses of smell and hearing were not helping them.

They had shuffled only twenty feet into a particularly lush field of six-foot-tall sorghum when a bright flash of orange flame and a thunderous boom cut the night air. The leading bull was knocked to his knees, a small dark hole appearing on the third wrinkle of his trunk, below his eyes. He died instantly. The other bull fled, deeply frightened, through the tall stalks, never to taste sorghum again.

The villagers, always on the ragged edge of survival, desperately needed to harvest the meager crops. They had alerted authorities after the first raid and pleaded for help after the second. The situation was dire for the village and the nearest authorities recognized it. An experienced game ranger with a heavy rifle, a .416 Rigby, was quickly dispatched. He knew that the elephants had been lightly peppered on the second raid, but he also knew that they would be back. He knew the direction from which the elephants would approach, and he knew that on this night, the breeze would not reveal his presence. He had the villagers stay in their huts with the dogs, no fires, no noise. The ranger also wanted to be able to use all of his senses. He positioned himself in the field of tall sorghum so that he could shoot shortly after the crop raiders entered. He thought they would come early as the full moon was rising in the east. And he waited as he had done so many times before.

He waited until the elephants were looming above him, only twenty feet away. Backlit by the rising moon, it was an easy shot for an experienced hunter. He could have, just as easily, shot the other young crop raider, but he thought that on this night, the young bull had received a strong message, a lesson, and would not raid village crops again.

Two and a half tons of elephant meat was a gift from the African heavens. It more than compensated for the significant crop losses and would produce some pleasant dietary changes. In the early light of the next day, the huge carcass was swarming with natives from villages up and down river. News travels quickly along the river highway and Azaan was surprised to see Rafiki and Yazid. He thought they had returned to Mozambique. But they were here with knives and baskets and the old Johnboat. By the next afternoon, little remained but large bones and offal that would be offered to the river and the crocodiles and the fish. Dozens of hastily built smoking racks covered the flat areas and mopane smoke filled the air. Great feasts of fresh meat were carried on before, during and after the butchering and smoking. Smoke cured elephant meat would enhance meals for months.

CHAPTER 20

THE CAMP

As the two men sat by the fire that night smoking the good, cured tobacco that the two traders, Rafiki and Yazid, had given them, the old man's concern was evident. He said, "Azaan, my son, I am bothered. I do not trust those men. They have offered to pay us to do something that they know, and we know is clearly illegal. I do not like the hushed conversations with some of the village men that they plainly do not want us to hear. They took a lot of unsmoked meat today; how will they keep it from spoiling? From the way you act around them, I suspect that you share my thoughts."

Azaan filled his pipe slowly and lit it before he spoke. "You know me too well. I do not trust them either and I am pretty certain that they are trying to secretly recruit some of the village men to trap for them. They know that you and I oppose what they are doing. Looking into the future, if the operation they are trying to organize in the villages along the river should get large enough and profitable enough, they could see you and I as dangerous enemies that could perhaps threaten their entire operation. Should things get to that stage, we could possibly be in serious danger. I don't think these guys are working alone."

"I agree with everything you have said. I think we need to know a lot more about them. I do not think you, as headman, should report them to the authorities at this time. We have little evidence of serious wrongdoing and some of the village men are making a little legal money with the fish and probably a bit of illegal money from trapping. I think, perhaps, you and I should pay their camp a visit, an uninvited, secret visit. Let us go as soon as we can so we can see what they do with a lot of uncured elephant meat. Let us leave in the early morning."

Venus was low in the western sky and the rising sun was only the slightest glimmer to the east when the two men left the village. From what they had been told, the traders camp was between Azaan's village and the closest downstream village, perhaps six or seven miles on the river but a substantially longer overland trek. Well-used animal trails led directly to and from the adjoining brush and forest to the river, but few trails followed the riverbank, so the short easy river miles were slow-going for the river-edge travelers.

The men knew that at this time of day the hippos would be returning to the river after an evening of foraging on the ever more distant grass. For the hippos, the river meant safety and sanctuary. Anything or anybody between them and this sanctuary was in the gravest of danger. Their trails to and from the river were pounded smooth and dusty but in the dark, the old man, the veteran tracker could not tell whether a trail was being used or not. They, therefore, had to pause frequently and listen for the sounds of the big bodies pushing through the tall growth. It was a dangerous place to make a mistake and they progressed slowly. Twice they waited quietly as one of the big animals passed in front of them moving surprisingly quickly. Morgan was carrying his spear, an old tribal tradition when danger might occur, but utterly useless against a hippo.

By the time the rising sun had cleared the eastern trees, the dangerous returning hippos were mostly all back in the river. But a new concern was developing. The patchy thick brush in the river bottom housed some notoriously aggressive tuskless cow elephants, which were now coming out of the bottom land to search for the few remaining apple ring acacia pods and to escape the annoying small bugs that pursued the moisture in the cows' eyes. The men were traveling through an open forest with a carpet of dry leaves. They could see and hear anything moving near them. They were only able to avoid the dangerous cows in this open area by lengthy detours, but the trip was taking much longer than they had anticipated.

Both men were glad for the presence of the other. The old man had been the head tracker for a professional hunter for more than twenty years and Azaan had been foraging in the forest for honey, nuts, melons, fruits, since he was a boy. They both knew the forest well and took what it gave them. Earlier the raspy bark of a bushbuck told them a leopard was finishing its hunt, later the screeching of a startled flock of guineas told the men that the leopard had headed south toward a high granite kopje. They surmised that the leopard was probably a female and possibly headed back to a den with cubs among the huge rocks.

They were nearing the end of their walk through the noisy dry leaves when Morgan abruptly stopped. The old tracker was staring intently at a spot about six feet ahead of him. He had been carrying his spear with the point up and the butt end down and being used as a walking stick. Slowly, he turned the shaft so that he held it by the butt end with the sharp spearhead out in front of him. Azaan was about to ask what he was doing when the old man suddenly swung the weapon in a low sweeping arc and the head of a thick snake popped into the air.

"A puff adder," Morgan said.

"I think I was looking right where he was," said Azaan, "but I could not see him. He is the same color as the leaves."

"I only saw him," said Morgan, "because there was a yellow leaf behind his head, and he was flicking his black tongue. If I had not seen that, I would have walked right into him."

The poacher's camp had been deliberately placed so that it was difficult to see from the main river. It was on the right bank, the west bank of a now dry tributary, above the first river bend, shielded by the tall river reeds and mopani scrub. The boats were secreted in a deep, dead-end bay behind a sandy island of twelve-foot reeds. The camp builders had obviously sacrificed good boat access to the camp for privacy, for secrecy. But when secrecy is the goal, mistakes cannot be made. And the camp builders made one. They did not know that the returning villager, weeks ago, had seen the big, covered boat that he then reported to his village headman. Anything out of place or different in this quiet, remote region where any news, was seized upon and discussed and analyzed, destroyed the attempt at secrecy, destroyed it even before the camp was built. The covered boat could have been easily hidden, but it wasn't.

From where they stood, Azaan and his father could see the hidden boats and they knew where the camp was from the sound of a gas engine, probably a generator. There were four boats: an aluminum canoe that had visited the village, a deep-hulled powerboat with a 50hp motor, the large, flat-bottomed cargo boat with a new 100hp Evinrude motor and the long dugout canoe. A wooden frame had been built to support a green shade and rain tarp; the big boat could be completely enclosed and protected from the elements. Two men in dirty shorts tinkered with the big Evinrude engine while a third man unloaded gas cans.

Drawing back into the forest, Azaan and Morgan walked a wide loop to put them at an elevated position to look down on the camp. The camp before them was laid out on a flat grassy area, ringed by tall trees. Six hammocks hung in the shade between the trees. Men slept or smoked in the hammocks, it being the hottest time of the day in the hottest time of the year. Shade tarps had been hung on frames over a number of crude, recently built tables. Several smokey little fires burned beneath racks layered with dark meat. A noisy generator powered a camouflage-painted refrigerator or freezer. At least a dozen camo-painted, eighty-quart coolers were stacked in the shade.

Little was stirring in the camp as the two watchers quietly retreated into the forest, satisfied that they had not been seen.

They walked for almost an hour as they headed back toward the village before the old man stopped to smoke his pipe and to talk.

Azaan said, "That is absolutely a commercial, game poaching camp, and it looks like it could process a lot more meat than it is getting from us and a couple of other fairly distant villages. The darker meat smoking on the racks is not fish, and I don't think it is the elephant meat that they took from us yesterday. But I wonder why they would be running the meat smoking fires this close to the river. It has a distinctive smell that anyone moving on the river would recognize."

"They are clever and experienced, my son; they know that the rising thermal air currents at this time of the day will carry the smoke up away from the river. In the evening, as the air cools the air currents will flow downhill, down the dry sand river valley by their camp, but they will have killed their smoking fires by then. Also, none of the river villagers would try to navigate this river in the dark."

"I should have known that," said Azaan, "I am embarrassed, it was not a good question. But what do you think of the generator and the freezer or refrigerator? Smoking and drying is by far the most common way and the easiest way to prevent meat spoilage?"

The old man slowly rose and tapped out his pipe and looked for a more comfortable place to sit. He spotted a small, moss-covered hump against a straight, thick tree and plopped down, his long legs angling comfortably downhill. "Well," he smiled and said, "I don't think all those camo-painted coolers are beer coolers. The smoked or dried meat is not to everyone's taste. The whites prefer fresh or frozen meat, and they eat it almost raw. These guys, these poachers probably have a buyer, or maybe a small market that serves the Europeans and Orientals. In the fast boat, with a big motor, it is probably only four or five hours into Mozambique where there is almost no river border control. Any control that might be there, these guys can easily bribe their way through. It would be meat for foreigners who do not want the dry, smoked game meat that we native river people have eaten, traded and sold since before anyone can remember. So, I kind of suspect, Azaan, that somewhere downstream of the camp probably in Mozambique is a foreigner who wants the fresh meat that he grew up with. He probably supplies the non-native community in his town. I, therefore, think that the guy who wants his fresh meat is probably running this whole operation. It is small now, but the boats, the camp, the approaches to the village men, suggests that this man has far grander plans, and that concerns me a lot and it should you too."

"Yes, I see it too father, but I am not sure how to deal with it."

"Neither am I," said the old man, frowning.

"But think of this," he said, "we are nearing the end of the dry season and there is a large concentration of game animals near the river. It can be the easiest hunting and trapping of the year. When the rains return in a few weeks, the antelope will disperse, following the new grass and budding shrubs. Most of the elephants will return to the high plateau far to the south. If the camp we watched is indeed the hub of a commercial poaching operation, I think we will very soon see a lot more activity from these guys. They cannot do it by themselves; they will have to try to get men from the river villages to help them, to hunt, trap and snare, to do their dirty work. I suspect we will have a visit from Rafiki and Yazid quite soon. And they will be interested in more than fish." The talk seemed to tire the old man, so he sat down again, filled his pipe, lit it and said, "I sure hope they bring some of that good tobacco. This stuff of yours, Azaan, burns my tongue."

CHAPTER 21

A LINE OF BUBBLES

The next morning, smoke from the burning grass filled the hot, dry air in every direction. It seemed hard to believe that the rains would ever come again. Several of the village men sat on the same stools they sat on every morning watching the boys and the women carrying buckets of water from the river to the always-thirsty gardens. It did not occur to any of them to offer to help. They looked down on a long, white sand beach where the garden waterers were filling their buckets. The water deepened gradually away from the beach; canoes and flat-bottomed boats could run up onto the sand and whoever was on board could get out without stepping into the water. To the right, downstream about fifty meters, where a seasonal stream entered the river, the water was deeper and darker, and was a place where keeled boats could reach the shore.

The river the men looked down on was a busy place in the morning. A herd of twenty or thirty hippos were mostly submerged, tired from their evening foraging in an area that was now more than a mile from the water. Farther downstream, an elephant herd was crossing the great river both walking and swimming. They had chosen their crossing point wisely—mostly shallow water with moderate flow rates where they had probably crossed many times before. Across the river, flying over the tall reeds, an agitated flock of snowy and cattle egrets announced the arrival of a herd of cape buffalo, numbering in the hundreds. More sinister elements were the crocodiles. Early, they were mostly in the water, but as the sun climbed higher in the sky, they crawled out of the water to warm themselves on the sand bars and sunlit banks. Azaan's village had not lost anyone to the crocs but the threat was always present. Most of the river villages had lost people to these silent, merciless killers.

Morgan was mostly silent this morning; he was not now a village member, so Azaan started the conversation. Not all of the men and women were there, but he told those that were there of his concerns and detailed the scouting of the downstream camp. "This appears to be a poaching camp designed for high volume meat processing and transport of both smoke-cured and fresh meat into Mozambique. Someone has invested a lot of money into this venture: boats, workers, refrigeration. What they appear to be doing is totally illegal, so at the border checkpoint authorities on both sides have probably been bribed. Our local rangers are probably the best trained and most prideful in all of Africa; they will not be bribed. Therefore, my friends, participation with these guys is at your own risk. The risk is large, but I realize that the potential reward is large as well. If you participate, I will, as your headman, make no effort to protect you. I will be on the side of the federal wildlife authorities." It appeared as though the older men nodded in approval and agreement. A few of the younger men were not at the meeting.

The old man thought Azaan's message to the village was the right one. The headman had no real authority. He told them what he knew and what he thought and with that information, he hoped they would make the prudent decision, the wise decision. But he well knew the temptations that were probably coming.

The old man said nothing as he listened and watched Kitafe and the other boys filling small buckets from the river. As he watched, the still sharp eyes of the old tracker noticed a long, straight line of bubbles on the river surface. The line of bubbles stopped where the water in front of the sand beach became too deep for him to see bottom, some thirty feet from the shoreline. He thought it could be one of the big catfish or maybe an otter, but it also might be a hunting crocodile attracted by the splashing of the boys with their little pails. From where the bubbles ended to the boys was too far for a surprise attack if indeed the bubbles were made by a hunting croc. As the old man walked down to warn the boys, a heavy plume of smoke from the burning grass fire cast the area into shade. When the smoke cleared, a long, dark shape had moved up into the shallow water. Now a single swipe of his powerful tail could propel the croc onto the beach, into the water carriers. The experienced killer was patient; he would wait until someone waded in a little farther than necessary. The boys were running ahead of the women coming back from the gardens. Morgan yelled at them to stop, just before they reached the water. At almost exactly the same moment, fourteen feet of death in waiting rocketed from ambush and landed with its head and little front legs on the beach, only feet from the boys. Before it could pull its thick hindlegs up under his body for a charge up the beach, a bunch of terrified, small boys were racing away. In seconds, the killer was back in the water, and a single tail swipe sent him out of sight. The old man was trembling; it was a life-threatening, close call for his grandson and all of the water haulers. The mothers were crying and hugging their little men. Water hauling ceased for the day.

The old man told the village men that he expects the traders, Rafiki and Yazid, to be paying them a visit. So, two village men left in their dugouts to check fishing lines. These are long, set lines with many hooks, baited with small fish, and the line is tied to a tree on shore. The fishermen have no way to preserve their catch, so any fish that they happen to hook is left on the line until a buyer arrives. When the fishermen return to the village, late in the afternoon, they bring eight of the big Vundu Catfish. They have been kept alive by a line that goes in their mouth and out below the gills and they are towed slowly back to the village to await a buyer. Their tow strings now become leashes that are tied to stream-side trees or bushes. The fishermen can only hope a buyer arrives before a croc or an otter finds their fish.

Early the next morning, the traders do arrive, this time in the fast powerboat. The big fish are quickly loaded and covered by a wet canvas sheet. They are exchanged for tobacco, coffee, tea, salt, whiskey, fishing line, hooks and some used children's clothing. No money is involved, because no one wanted the local currency. This time, the quick happy one, Yazid, steers the conversation, "Our clients would also like some dark meat, animal meat, especially antelope and monkey. We would want to obtain the monkeys intact, if possible. I know that there is a concern here about the legality of trading in game meat, but I think it is your individual choice to make. So, to avoid any confrontation or conflict, we dropped off some wire snares and some leg-hold traps down the river under the large baobab tree past the end of the sandy beach. Set them both to catch legs. Neck-caught animals usually die, and the meat can spoil in the heat. They stay alive for days if caught by the leg. We will return in three days."

The trade goods were welcome, but the old man knew that they came with a price that would challenge a man's honesty and integrity in the next several days, and he knew other villages were being exposed to the same temptations. Proceeds from poaching gave men easy access to things that were usually difficult, even impossible, to get. There were lots of animals, what would a few traps hurt? The old man hated both; all sorts of animals wandered into snares, and the traps with a leg-caught animal meant days, weeks, even months of suffering for perhaps an unintended victim.

Morgan, who was born and lived most of his life in the village, gathered together who he could of the small village, and began, "We know what the traders want now. But they will want more. Mark my words; now they want fish and meat, and we are giving them some of that. Next, they will want more of those, and then they will want other things. You are entering, if you choose to, a most dangerous situation. I ask you to consider what has been and will be most important for you and for your family. By European or most African standards, you are poor. But through hard work, you have what you most need. Every year your family is fed, you are sheltered, and you owe no one anything. Your kids are educated by the parents and the elders. They know the river and the forest and their place and obligation in the family. You have what most of so-called society most wants. Believe me, I have seen the other side." When he finished, he knew he had dumped a lot of his moralistic thoughts on them. They came from his heart though, from the man he was, and they mostly accepted what he said.

"So," a few of the villagers probably thought, "who is this old guy, preaching moral guidance? What would trapping a few animals, catching a few more fish really hurt?" But deep inside, the old man had aroused their conscience. In the small society that was this village, their code of honor was an unwritten ethic that permeated their lives as it had since the beginning. It happened naturally in isolated villages like this. No one had anything to be envious of, there was nothing to compete for except respect. If someone needed help, someone was usually there to give it. An influx of money and goods would certainly bring cultural changes, but probably not good ones. In spite of their misgivings, the temptation was large.

CHAPTER 22

HIPPOS

"I like walking with you," Kitafe said. "I like being with you in the bush and you answer all my questions. You ask me questions about what I am seeing and hearing and learning and that makes me think more seriously than if I were alone. Let's go look at the hippos; tell me about them. Tell me what you see and what I don't see."

The old man was pleased. He patiently considered and told him, "Many people, but probably not river villagers, think that hippos kill more people than any other African animal. They are huge and can be extremely dangerous. The old bulls with a harem of cows, seem to always be in a bad mood. They will turn over a small boat if it enters their territory and attack the occupants. If someone gets between any hippo and its sanctuary in the water, the person could easily be trampled. Sometimes people just get too close."

"But they are not hunters. Killings related to hippos are mostly accidental, someone is in the wrong place at the wrong time. Crocs, on the other hand, kill, I think, far more people deliberately than hippos kill by accident. Hunting is what crocs do, and they are patient, deadly and efficient. They plan an attack; hippos mainly just accidentally stumble into and onto an unlikely someone. I also think a lot more people die from snake bites."

"Let's watch the group that has just come back from a long evening, foraging on the distant grass. The riverside grass has been grazed back from the river more than a mile. This morning the air is cool, almost cold, so I think we will see the hippos go right into the river because that water is a lot warmer than the air."

"Are the groups of hippos one large, related family like the elephants?" Kitafe asked.

"Good question, small one" the old man replied, "but, no, I don't think they are. Although when you make me think about it, I guess I don't really know. They show little, if any, affection for each other. They don't seem to communicate very well, and they all look the same, except for their size. That big bull fiercely defends his herd of girls and kids from any other bulls. Fights with other bulls are frequent, long and usually bloody. Hippos live a long time, 25, maybe thirty years so I guess I'd have to say, I don't think a herd bull wins all of his fights for twenty years. So probably several fathers have offspring in this herd. But you know the hippo bulls are not bad fathers; they ferociously defend the entire pod from threats for as long as one is dominant. The elephant bull, on the other hand, drops by for a conjugal visit and he is off for greener pastures. He plays little part in the family."

"Kitafe, my favorite little traveling companion, there is something that I wish you would think about when we are watching and trying to understand what the animals are doing and thinking. They do not think or react like people do and we do not think and react as they do. Our people living in the bush pretty much know this. Foreigners, young people, city people mostly do not. Let me give you a made-up example: lions attack a buffalo, and the buffalo gets away. Naïve onlookers are happy for the escaping buffalo or sad for the hungry, panting lion. I would suspect that the buffalo simply puts it behind her and wants to go get a drink. She isn't angry at the lion or joyful that she got away. It is a memory, and she is not thinking ahead. Same sort of thing with the lioness: 'missed this one but I'll try again another time.' It was an event with little lasting emotion for either of them. What I am awkwardly trying to tell you is that human feeling and emotions relate poorly to understanding animal behavior."

This was a long, heavy talk for a seven-year-old to process, but he felt the sincerity in the old man's message and "they aren't like us" came through clearly. It was a message he would not forget. But he thought that maybe elephants were somehow different, and he was anxious to talk about them with his grandfather. But now was not the time.

CHAPTER 23

COOL WATER

October is the hottest month. Day after day temperatures rise to over 100 degrees. Rangers and villagers burn the dry grass so that the new grass will have room to grow when the rains finally come. For the tribes and the animals, it is an unpleasant time of heat, smoke and fire. Weeks of thunder and lightning proceed the rains, igniting yet more fires.

The elephants stay close to the river under the dwindling shade of the tall trees during the hottest time of the day. Cool river water is a welcome relief from the cloud of bugs and the scorching sun, so the elephants are often in it. They sometimes seek out the soft, moist river plants; but mostly they simply seem to enjoy just being in the water. They fill their trunks and don't seem to care if half of it misses their mouth. The dust they sprayed on their backs after the last bath is now caked mud, but they want fresh mud. Endless trunkfuls of river water are sprayed on their backs and along their sides to wash off the old dirt. It is a daily recurring process that the big animals seem to enjoy.

For the smaller members of the herd, this is a wonderful time. They trot around butting each other, tangling their little trunks and trying to figure out how to use them. Behati can pull up clumps of grass from the mud, like Njeri, but he can't seem to get it into his mouth. No matter, he can't eat it anyway. In the water, the little ones happily splash around. They watch the big ones fill their trunks and spray themselves and try to imitate. It isn't working but they are beginning to use their trunks to drink. At times, even some of the big elephants want to play with each other, pushing, tangling trunks, completely submerging. The old man had told Kitafe that to him elephant culture seemed more advanced than that of most of the other animals. Huto had returned to the breeding herd for what seemed to be a social visit. He was calm, not aggressive, and he didn't smell bad, and the ladies did not seem to mind his presence.

THE PRICE

The large powerboat pushed slowly up the south bank of the Zambezi allowing Rafiki and Yazid to scan the bank, to assess animal populations. By the end of the dry season, animals concentrated near water and the poachers were pleased with what they saw. Impala were especially numerous, but there were good numbers of some of the large antelope in particular eland and kudu. They had no way to deal with the massive cape buffalo whose large herds were scattered along both banks, but they were something to think about for next year. Elephants were everywhere, in and out of the water. Once they caught a brief glimpse of the massive tusks of Huto and they saw several lesser bulls.

An urgency marked their upcoming visit to Azaan's village. Every day they heard the distant thunder and, in the evening, saw the jagged streaks of lightning to the south and west. The rainy season was fast approaching, and the flooding tributary streams and muddy trails would greatly restrict and possibly end the poaching season. Yazid and Rafiki needed to push the river villagers to step up their trapping. They brought more snares, more traps and a .300 Weatherby Magnum rifle for the big antelope.

For the poachers, the harvest season was upon them, but they sorely needed help, help only the villagers could supply. Azaan received them coolly and Morgan sat away, not part of the meeting, but within hearing distance. Yazid explained that with the coming of the rains, the hunting and trapping season would soon end, and they had large demands for meat and other products in Mozambique. If the villagers were to help them, they would have to work much harder than they had been. "We have seen the concentration of animals along the river. I have left more traps and snares and a heavy rifle and ammunition where I left things before and I hope you can help us." Then, he asked two boys to go to the boat and bring up the boxes in the front of the boat. Whiskey, tobacco, sweets, but also real necessities. Then, he went on, "If there are other things you need or would like, I can also get those, but not until next season." Then, he went on, "I have a strong market for some other things too ... pangolins, civets (both of them whole), crocodile skins, ivory, lion parts." Morgan cringed and thought, "So this is how it works; this is what they have really wanted all along."

The village men brought him some fish and a few small antelopes, and they were paid as they wished. But all knew that a larger pickup would occur downriver, out of sight of the village. They also knew that the traps, snares and rifles would be picked up. Two of the young village men had not been seen for more than a week and both had had previous minor legal issues. They had parents in the village, and both were pleasant, respectful, young members of the community. But they felt confined, isolated and restricted and were looking for something different, for a way out. Rafiki and Yazid could perhaps provide such an exit.

The boys met Rafiki and Yazid below the village and gave them the animals they had caught in their snares and traps. They had more game than the entire village had trapped. The traders were pleased and asked for even more. If the boys could learn to shoot a rifle, the big eland and kudu would be easy prey. Yazid would school them this very day on using the heavy 300 Weatherby Magnum rifle. He took them far downriver, beyond earshot of the village. The young men knew nothing of guns and initially thought it was the loud noise that killed. But they learned quickly and in a few hours were shooting well enough to hit large animals. Yazid knew that they would improve, and that same afternoon dropped them off with the gun and shells back at the place where he had met them.

The newly armed hunters did not want the sound of a shot to reach the village, so they would hunt another two miles further downstream. They slept on the ground with only a tiny fire and arose as the full moon was setting and the rising sun brightened the bottom of the dark eastern sky. Because dry leaves covered the ground, they knew that stalking would not be effective. The best strategy would be to wait along a game trail and try to shoot something coming to drink at the river. On their first day with the rifle, they waited less than an hour before they heard a peculiar clicking sound, which they knew to be coming from the ankles of approaching eland. They stood behind a tall termite mound, and as the massive antelope passed less than fifty feet in front of them, a single shot from the 300 Weatherby Magnum dropped a young bull. Only when they came up onto the antelope did they realize how large an eland really is; this young bull would weight nearly 1000 pounds. Although they were close to the river and a pickup spot, they would need to cut the animal into movable sized pieces. Many hours later, a neat stack of fresh, dark meat lay on a bed of reeds, beside the river, covered by more reeds. The boys would wait for a pickup, which they hoped would come the next morning. Blood oozed from the pile of cooling flesh and seeped into the slow-moving current.

Early the next morning, they spotted Rafiki and Yazid's boat heading downstream. As it had picked up quite a bit of game and fish at their village and another village farther upstream, there was not enough space to load the eland meat. Yazid told the boys that he would drop his cargo at their big camp and come back for the eland later that day. Little fish, attracted by the blood in the water attracted bigger, predatory fish, especially tigerfish.

The deep-keeled power boat's motor seemed to be struggling as it approached the hunters and the stacked meat. Rafiki and Yazid got out into knee deep water and began to rapidly load meat into the rear of the boat, wading to shore to take large pieces of dripping meat from the hunters. No one noticed the intermittent line of small bubbles steadily approaching from downriver. When the loading was complete, Rafiki raised the outboard and waded to the back of the boat to remove a tangle of weeds from the prop. He was standing in waist-deep water when the crocodile, which had followed the drifting bloodstream, powered into him. His legs were close together as he stood to clear the prop and the powerful jaws clamped down on both knees together, crushing bone and severing both femoral arteries. In seconds, fourteen feet of remorseless killer was dragging the still-struggling Rafiki to meet his maker at the bottom of the river. A dazed Yazid dropped the motor and powered down the river with the cargo that had cost his best friend his life.

Three days later, Yazid returned to the village with another man. This man was different from the smiling, happy Rafiki and Yazid. His skin was light, but not white; he had narrow eyes and thin lips and he did not smile. He spoke English with an unfamiliar accent as he surveyed the cargo they would be picking up. In addition to the Vundu Catfish and several small antelopes, were two civets, a young baboon and a 25-pound piece of elephant tusk that one of the men found near a decomposing elephant carcass.

The stranger was obviously the man in charge, and he exchanged common trade goods for the animals. Then, he turned to the piece of ivory and astounded the onlookers with his offer to purchase it. It was for far more goods or money than any of them had ever seen. And it was for only a part of one tusk. He subtly made it clear that he would buy any ivory they could provide. *So, this is what they really wanted all along*, thought Morgan.

The stranger noted the old man's obvious disapproval and said to him, "Do you not want better things for these villagers?"

"Yes," Morgan replied, "I do want better things for these people. But I am thinking along the lines of access to medical supplies and care, access to education for the children, maybe an electrical generator, maybe a powerboat. I do not think more whiskey or tobacco or radios and flashlights or the guns that they could buy, would necessarily be better for the village. I have told them of my thoughts and my concerns about dealing with your people. You confirmed all of my worst fears when you offered so much for ivory. These are good, simple people living honestly and happily with their families. I wish you people had never appeared."

The thin stranger turned from Morgan and said to the villagers, "We will be back to trade in three days."

The village boys carried the animals and the piece of ivory to the boat and Yazid turned the boat downriver. He stopped briefly to talk with the young hunters of the eland and said he would return in two days. As Yazid and the stranger approached the big poachers' camp, the stranger said, "We need to get rid of the old man. You do it and do it soon. The villagers must not know that we were involved. I will pay you well." Yazid gasped at the thought; he was horrified.

CHAPTER 25

CHAO

Chao Fang is thirty-six years old; he has been in Africa nearly nine years. His parents were both in the military, so in their minds, military service for their only son was nearly compulsory. As he was single, spoke fluent English, and his family was not of the military elite, he was posted to a huge African mining concession as a security officer. Although he did not come from a background of wealth, Chao was accustomed to a somewhat gentile lifestyle. He had few friends; most thought him at best as distant and aloof, and at worst as unpredictable and threatening.

The copper mining region was a ravaged wasteland. Decades of ruthless disregard for any environmental concerns left a landscape littered with heaps of mine waste, heavily polluted water and a great many impoverished workers. Chao performed his security functions easily; there was little crime other than persistent minor theft. He did not understand any of the native languages and was thus involved with the workers only through their headmen who maybe could speak a bit of English.

For Chao, the ravaged mining region was also a cultural wasteland. He was an educated, oriental man with no one to talk to. Ready access to a vehicle allowed him to escape the depression the mine generated in his soul, and he traveled widely on his off days. After he had been in the area for two or three years, he found his way to the Benguela Wetlands, an enormous swampy area in the northeast part of the country. He found the seasonably flooded wetland to be a fresh, untarnished oasis in his adopted African home. It abounded with birds and animals; bird songs replaced the roar of diesel engines. Natives from scattered villages harvested huge numbers of small fish with nets fashioned from mesh sheeting designed for malarial protection and which was widely distributed by well-meaning, but poorly informed foreign charities.

After one of his visits to the wetland, he mentioned to one of his supervisors where he had been and the great number of birds and animals. The man then casually asked Chao if he happened to see a shoebill. Chao answered, "I don't know. What do they look like?" "They are a large blue-grey wading bird with an enormous bill shaped like a shoe. They will stand motionless in the water for long periods of time before striking violently at a fish or snake or frog. They are most distinctive; they look like no other bird." Chao told him that he was pretty certain he had seen them.

The supervisor then quietly said, "I have a friend, a wealthy friend who has a large collection of the smaller local animals and some birds. The most unique and distinctive bird in this area is the shoebill. If you could capture one or arrange for one to be captured, this man would pay very well." Compared to the drudgery of mine security, this sounded like a welcome relief, maybe even some rare fun, with a potential big payday.

Chao immediately began learning what he could about the iconic shoebill from the mining company's modest library. Then, he began thinking of how to catch one. In less than a week, he thought he knew how to do it. The birds build nests on islands of floating vegetation starting at the end of the rainy season. Both parents share incubating and also cooling the eggs when necessary. They both share raising the chicks, ensuring that once found, a nest would have adult shoebills on it for a matter of months.

Chao's plan was to get one of the fishermen with a net to drift quietly up to a floating nest, in the dark, and throw the net over whoever was on the nest. Chao instructed two of the local fishermen in fashioning a large replica of a fishing cast net. It was to be round, about ten feet across, made of strong, wide mesh, with weights around the edges. It was designed to open up to its full diameter as it was thrown with the weights, pulling the edges down over anything it encircled. It took a strong man to throw the mesh trap, but the throws would be short.

Although it took a few days to locate a suitable nest, the plan worked perfectly the very first night they tried. However, the men were frightened by the fearsome bill of the big bird and while trying to roughly force it into a capture bag, a wing was broken. When Chao saw the injured bird the next morning, he erupted in rage at the two fishermen. His wild screaming frightened them badly as he threatened to beat them. This he thought better of as both men were powerfully built and much larger than him. When Chao finally regained his composure, he paid the men a bit of money and told them to replace the injured bird near its nest and capture another. In the early morning hours a few days later, Chao was able to deliver a fine, mature shoebill to a heavy man sitting beside an open door in a darkened car. The man passed Chao an envelope and asked if he could get other birds. The money was more than Chao made at the mine in three months and so began the poaching career of one Chao Fang.

One night, a few weeks later, he packed his things and walked to the motor pool. A young, uninformed woman who was guarding the motor pool smiled and asked Chao for his authorization receipt when he requested the Ford F-250 pickup. Without a word, he smashed a hard fist into her face and continued to beat her into unconsciousness. Then, he calmly loaded his things, including a 30-caliber rifle into the truck, filled it with gas and disappeared into the African night.

CHAPTER 26

THATCHING GRASS

For the villagers, it is a busy time of the year. Fields and gardens are harvested and prepared for the coming planting season. Wood is gathered and the kiln prepared for making charcoal. But perhaps most important task is rethatching and patching the roofs of the huts before the arrival of the seasonal rains, which would soon be upon them.

The thatching grasses along the river are now fully grown, and ready to be cut. Early one morning as the sun is a yellow half disk peaking over the horizon, Azaan picked up his big knife, some long lengths of homemade twine and headed down the river in the long dugout, which his father had carved many years before.

He would have liked to take his oldest son with him, but with the load of thatching grass, there was not enough room. It is early November, and the river is at its lowest as Azaan drifts carefully searching for a place where the grass is tall and close to the water.

The river is his backyard, and he notices everything. He sees a large area of disturbed sand above the riverbank and knows that a crocodile recently opened her nest to let out the hatchling baby crocs. Among the eggshells, he sees the huge, three-toed tracks of a goliath heron and thinks the big bird probably ate some of the late hatchlings.

Farther down, a wide muddy tunnel through the tall reeds shows him where the hippos leave and return from their nightly grazing area. The hippos are now far out in the river and pose no threat to him. On a wide sand bar, he sees where jackals have dug up a river turtle's nest and probably eaten all her eggs.

A low rumbling sound and breaking branches tell him that an elephant herd has recently drunk and is slowly returning to the shade of the riverside forest. They are beyond his view and moving away. Their spore will tell Azaan about the size of the herd, what they have been eating, whether there are calves, which would make the herd much more dangerous, and particularly if there are any big bulls with them. He beaches his dugout and examines the soft mud: a small herd, ten to fifteen cows several young ones, and the enormous tracks of what appears to be a huge bull. He notes depressions in the sand where the bull had rested his tusks. Then, he notices something unusual; one of the small calves has a straight-line scar that goes completely across its foot. He will mention this to his father.

Azaan does not cut the tall coarse reeds for his roof, but instead chooses some fine, dense grass a little less than waist high. He tries to cut it all the same length. He and Anoona will tie the grass into tight bunches before stacking it onto their roof in overlapping layers, starting at the bottom. It is work that they have done many times before; they have always enjoyed working together on their roof. The work is time consuming but easy and Azaan likes to listen to Anoona who always sings while she thatches.

The distant rumbling thunder of the approaching rains is pierced by the shrieks of a pair of hunting fish eagles as Azaan slowly paddles the heavily loaded dugout back upstream toward his village. The first few drops of the new wet season hit him as he unloads his first load of thatching grass in front of his little house. The cold rain makes him shiver for the first time in months.

CHAPTER 27

THE HUNT

Two days later, as he approached his meeting with the young hunters, Yazid was troubled thinking about what he had been asked to do. Kill the old man! Yazid had never killed anything larger than a chicken, much less a person. He considered himself a simple river boatman. He moved all sorts of goods on the river. He thought that some of the cargo he carried was probably illegal but the penalties, if he were to be caught, were mild. The penalties for killing a man were horrific, death by hanging or by a rifle shot or a life sentence in a sweltering African prison notorious for their filthy conditions and the short life spans of the residents. Besides, he thought, in our culture the old man is a respected elder. His thoughts are always taken seriously and his response to the unsmiling man was the right message to him and to the villagers. Yazid thought, *I think I like him; I know I respect him. But he probably doesn't like me at all.* This time Yazid brought a heavy 375 H&H rifle to his meeting with the young hunters. He wanted to shoot a bull elephant. Huto, who he had glimpsed twice, was his first choice, but two of the other bulls in the little bachelor herd carried tusks of 50 or 60 pounds each and they would certainly suffice. Huto's band was some distance east of the hunters, away from the village, and out of earshot. Yazid would be the one to shoot the big rifle; he did not want the powerful recoil to be a factor in the young hunters' first attempt at an elephant. The two hunters had shadowed the little herd for more than a week and they knew their daily routine; when they drank and fed, when and where they rested, what ivory was carried by each.

They would wait until the elephants finished their morning watering and had moved into the shade of the forest. Because of the carpet of dry, crackling leaves, the three men paddled a canoe downstream to where the elephants had left the river. The big animals' trail into the forest shade was damp from the dripping bodies and the hunters approached nearly soundlessly on the damp trail. As the animals glided slowly among the trees and bushes, the hunters caught a quick look at the massive tusks of Huto. The herd was completely unaware of the hunters and Yazid thought they should get closer. But an occasional light breeze over their right shoulder was worrisome. If it shifted only slightly to the left, it would carry their scent to the herd, and they would surely spook. Suddenly, all herd movement ceased; the elephants sensed something. Ears fanned, trunks waved. Yazid had a shot at which he thought to be the shoulder of an elephant with ivory peeking through the heavy brush.

At the shot, the previously quiet forest exploded into a cacophony of trumpeting, roaring elephants crashing through the thick brush. The target animal was hit, and it had tusks, but it was not Huto. As soon as the danger from stampeding, vengeful elephants was past, the hunters took up the blood trail of the wounded animal. There was a great deal of blood; the animal was hard hit, but it was not the bright frothy liquid, which would indicate a quickly fatal lung shot. From the amount of blood, it was obvious that the wounded animal would die, but he could likely walk a long way before he did.

The sun was already high, there wasn't a cloud to be seen, as the hunters prepared for a long, hot walk. They carried only their water bottles, the rifle, and an ax. The blood trail was heavy and easy to follow; the sweating hunters followed at a near trot. In less than an hour, they were pleased to see an ever-increasing number of vultures spiraling toward the ground. The elephant had apparently tired and leaned against a tree, before expiring and sliding to the ground.

The big animal was laying on his chest and belly exposing his right tusk to the sky. The left tusk was partly under his head. None of the men had ever removed a tusk before, but the sharp little ax was the perfect tool for the job. It was slow, careful work for the ivory got progressively thinner and more delicate as they worked up toward its root. At least a hundred vultures surrounded them in the surrounding trees. Several white-backed vultures had spotted the wounded elephant as it stumbled uphill away from the single gunshot that hammered its midsection. The grim birds were experts regarding the dead and the dying. Jackals and marabou storks joined the always hungry vultures, waiting for the men to leave.

The salvaged tusk was short, thick and heavy, at least 50 pounds. It was surprisingly clean and white from frequent trips to the river. As the other tusk was partly under the bull's head, it was impossible to reach with the little ax. All three had heard that if the carcass sat for five or six days, the natural processes would work, and it could probably be pulled free with little or no cutting. The three men alternated carrying the tusk downhill to the waiting boat. They would sleep well tonight.

On the sixth day after the hunt, the light-colored man who did not smile returned with Yazid to retrieve the other tusk. The young hunters went with them and the quiet grim man carried the heavy rifle with hopes of shooting another bull elephant, especially Huto. The man's greed was unmistakable as he set a fast pace toward the carcass. Putrid wafts of air reached them long before they could see what remained of the fallen giant. Vultures filled the trees; there must have been a couple hundred and blackbacked jackals darted among the trees. Yazid and the pale man hurried ahead into the increasing stench, but the young hunters paused. Something was not right; why were the vultures in the trees and not feeding on the ripe carcass? Why were the jackals not trying to eat? They cautioned Yazid with a soft whistle and the two men halted and returned to the young hunters. They were close but they still could not see the remains through the trees and brush. Quietly, the men circled around the area where the bull lay until they reached a low hill and could look down onto the scene from some hundred meters away. What they saw shocked them

ALLAN LARSON

to their cores and Yazid and the pale man knew that the hunters caution had probably saved their lives. Lions nearly covered what remained of the big body; others lay nearby panting in the hot sun; several cubs sniffed at the ripe feast. At least fifteen, maybe twenty lions were feeding or, to judge from their bloody faces, had recently fed. Had Yazid and the other man suddenly appeared at close range, a deadly charge was a near certainty. No one wanted to get even a step closer.

It was a somber crew that returned to the empty boat that afternoon. The pale man then decided that in two more days only the young hunters should return for the tusk. Hopefully the lions would have had enough and left in search of a fresher meal or gone to the river for a long drink after days of gorging. But he would not send the rifle with the two.

CHAPTER 28

CONFESSION

On the morning of the second day, after the visit to the carcass and the lions, Yazid powered the boat up to the village to pick up whatever fish or game animals the villagers would have to trade. There wasn't much and Yazid sensed there wouldn't be much more. Bringing the pale man to the village was a mistake. Although Yazid did not think of it that way at the time, it was a serious error in judgement. He and Rafiki could talk and laugh and bargain with these people because of a shared ethnic, social, traditional lifestyle. The stranger would not relate at all except in the simple terms of what he wanted and what he would pay. He was so grim and unsmiling that the villagers felt he did not like them, and there really wasn't much about him for them to like either. Theirs was a culture where money was not the great equalizer; and this was something the pale trader would never understand.

Yazid's life had always been a happy, carefree one. He rarely worried about anything. He had friends and good parents, and sort of a girlfriend. But now he had gotten himself into a situation that he did not like. One that had also cost him his best friend. He knew that Azaan did not care for him because of what he was asking his villagers to do, but Yazid knew what he had to do, and do it soon. He found Azaan tying bundles of thatching grass and told him, "I must talk to your father. Is he here?"

"No, he and Kitafe are fishing, but he should be back soon."

Yazid said, "I would like to talk to him alone."

The old man and Yazid sat beside each other on a heavy log, each looking out onto the river, below the boat. Yazid started, "I know that you don't like what I have been doing lately. And honestly, I don't like me much these days either. I am flaunting the laws and trying to get others to join me. It may sound like an excuse, but I fell under another's influence, who I have now come to recognize for what he truly is. It is only about the money for him; nothing else matters. This is the thin man who came to the village, the man who you spoke to about village values and culture. His name is Chao; he represents an oriental trading company. They want to trade everything from bushmeat to pangolin scales to elephant ivory, and everything in between. They do not care how any of this is obtained. But you and your influence with the people of the village are a threat to his grand plan for this entire region. He is an evil man. He has asked me to kill you or arrange for you to be killed. If he had any idea that I was talking to you about anything at all, I have little doubt that I would be immediately expendable. Honored elder, I need your guidance; what should I do?"

The old man very slowly packed his pipe and lit it as he thought about how to answer the troubled man's question. "This does not come as a total surprise to me, Yazid," he quietly replied. "I tried to provoke a reaction, but definitely not this one. The way I see it, there are at least three of us who may be at risk: you, me and, unfortunately, my grandson maybe also Azaan. I believe these are thoroughly ruthless people who have few limits. You are the easiest to shield. You simply disappear to your home village, wherever that is, and sit there quietly. I cannot protect myself or Kitafe from a long-range rifle shot. Azaan and I know the forest; he does not, but he could have some people that do. Before you return to your home village, try to see if Chao has any people who know the bush well enough to be a threat. And absolutely make Chao know that you are still with him."

A heavy thunder shower drummed down on Yazid as he met the hunters with the ivory tusk, who both expected to be well paid for a dangerous retrieval. The lions were gone but the hunters didn't know that, and the risk was huge. Yazid had no authority or money to pay them. When no money was offered, the hunters, young though they were, thought they had been cheated badly; they immediately thought to get even. They had made three long uphill treks, carried tusks and other gear down, and gotten nothing, and they knew something of the extremely high value of ivory on the river markets. This casual, little business relationship with Yazid and Chao was over, but the young hunters held a high card. Chao, the poacher-in-chief, needed them. They just needed a way to use the high card. That evening the two men sat quietly before a small fire, eating their mealies with a little elephant trunk meat, thinking that Yazid was still Chao's loyal worker. They both wanted to go back to their village, but they knew the poachers needed them, and that gave them a chance to somehow even the score. But they had no plan.

News travels quickly and easily along the river and Azaan's villagers were soon aware of the elephant kill, the tusk retrievals and the wayward boys not being paid. The village did not like the whole situation, but they thought along the lines of the ancient parable, "Honor among thieves must prevail. You do not cheat your partner in crime."

CHAPTER 29

THE HAND

The carmine bee eaters were massing along the vertical mud bank on the south side of the Zambezi. They were there in the hundreds, returning to old holes and drilling new holes, where they would lay their eggs and raise their young. Morgan wanted Kitafe to see them, these the loveliest of the beautiful bee eater clan. As they glided quietly along, back from the mud bank, the birds were everywhere, on the ground and in the air, their brilliant plumage radiating in the low morning sun.

The old man knew that Kitafe's sense of hearing was extraordinary and when the boy said, "Grandfather, someone follows," he quickened their pace and paused to the side of the trail behind a thick bush and waited. The one who silently followed was suddenly aware of the point of Morgan's spear touching his throat. The follower was a heavily tattooed, dark, thick man, carrying a rifle, low in his right hand.

"Why do you follow us?" Morgan asked.

"We are simply watching the birds." The man sneered, raised his rifle, and snarled, "I am going to take the boy, old man." The spearhead flashed from the man's neck to his wrist, and a rifle and right hand dropped to the ground. The thick man gasped and vomited.

"Tell me who sent you, or I will let you bleed out here," came the quiet voice of the old man.

"Chao, Chao, Chao," croaked the voices of the now one-handed man, "he sent me, but he will send others." The man quickly wrapped his shirt around the pulsating stump and hurried back in the direction of his camp, Chao's camp. Although he didn't know what he would do with it, Morgan picked up the rifle. Others would find the hand. Kitafe looked down at the blood oozing from the hand and he too vomited.

CHAPTER 30

BE CAREFUL

When they returned to the village, Morgan told Azaan what had happened. He said, "If not for Kitafe's superb hearing, I might not be telling you this." He did not tell his son of the conversation with Yazid, thinking that the fewer people that knew of a potentially deadly secret, the better for all. It was most worrying to Azaan that the man currently with one hand had told his father that others would come.

There seemed to be only two options for the old man and the boy. They could return to Morgan's home village, several long walking days away or they could stay in Azaan's village in a state of the highest awareness until they could develop some kind of a survival plan. The old man's dignity, his honor was at stake. He would never run even if it increased the risk to Kitafe.

There were few secrets in a small bush village and within only a few hours, everyone knew of the attempt to kidnap Kitafe and the kidnapper's gruesome fate. For the next few days, it was the only thing they talked about. Was the man crazy? Did he have a curse on him that could only be removed with the offering-up of a child? Was the child cursed? Or did he think the old man could pay a ransom?

Superstition runs deeply in the African psyche, and when the severed hand could not be found, a sinister, spiritual underworld was widely believed to be involved. Witch doctors are the interface, the connection, between the dark underworld of spirits and demons, and the common man, the innocent farmer, to whom spirits and curses are as real as his wife and children. Witch doctors curse people and they remove curses. They don't do either for nothing. Dealing with curses is integral in a village's culture. If, for instance, a man believes his wife is fooling around with another man, the aggrieved husband may pay a witch doctor to put a curse on the other man. The victim of the curse may not know he has been cursed, but the first time he has a headache or a cold or any minor malady, and he learns he has been cursed; he thinks this is just the beginning. It will only get worse. His fear and worry about the curse, compounds what was initially simply a harmless discomfort. He does what he has to do to have the curse removed.

Dry lightning played across the southern sky far across the glassy river, harkening the approach of the rains. Azaan's harvest work was finished; some seeds had been planted, to be harvested next year. A bit of roof thatching remained, but he had idle time,

time to sit and smoke his pipe and to have the serious talk he needed to have with his father. They both knew that the old man's life was in real danger. After Morgan told Azaan of Yazid's painful confession, they both thought that they could trust him, but he had been on the other side leaving the men with some lingering uneasiness.

A narrow footpath followed the south bank of the river for tens, if not hundreds of miles, loosely connecting the river villages. It was used for some trading of needed goods, but it was treated mostly as social corridor between villages. Nearly every day someone or a group would pass or stop to visit at the village. Azaan's wife in fact was from an upriver village some fifteen miles away. He first saw her when she was ten or twelve years old, passing his village on the path, when he was sixteen or eighteen. By the time she was fifteen, Azaan thought she was the most beautiful girl he had ever seen. He was a shy, extremely shy, teenager but he had to have her. First meetings, follow-ups with parents seemed easy for her. For him it was the scariest place he had ever been. She steered him easily through it all.

Late one afternoon, a stranger came up the trail form downriver. He was a short, gaunt older man of the most unusual appearance. He was heavily tattooed with several strands of large beads around his neck. The bedraggled remains of a leopard skin circled his waist with a bit of the tail still attached. He wore a once-white Rolling Stones tee shirt and a hat fashioned from the skin of a baboon's head and face. He explained to the quickly gathering villagers that he was old, tired and hungry and could not go farther. He would have to stay with them. He seemed to have brought nothing except an animal skin bag that hung from a strap around his neck, a sleeping mat, a blanket and a water bottle.

The villagers took him in, fed him, sheltered him and tried to talk to him. "Where are you going? Where are you coming from?" Those questions got no answers.

"I come from where I was needed. I go to where I am needed, and I am needed here. You have an evil spirit in your village. I have come to rid you of him." A witch doctor had arrived, and Morgan and Azaan knew it was probably not by accident.

The old man had been around witch doctors all his life. He thought that they brought little or nothing of value, but their influence among the brush people was enormous. Morgan knew that he alone had a dangerous adversary, and from his scant possessions, he knew where he had come from. This cunning little creature, designed to charm his way into the village would try, in some way, to kill him.

"Kitafe," he said quietly, "Let's take a walk. I wish to talk. I think I will need your help."

They walked down the trail from which the witch doctor first appeared. "I do not trust that tattooed old man, and not just because he is a witch doctor. I think he must have come from the poacher's camp, a few miles downriver since he did not carry any food or things to sustain him. The poachers know that I don't like them, and they hate me. He has been sent to do me harm, serious harm. I cannot watch him continuously; therefore, I would like you and the boys to watch him and tell me if he does anything strange or unusual, better yet just tell me whatever he does. His appearance is so strange, he probably expects people, especially children, to stare at him. But do not get close to him."

For two days, the little man puttered around the village. He cast minor spells, removed perceived curses, interpreted the origin or cause of curses and ills, explained why someone or something had died. In his world, nothing that happened was due to natural causes and the villagers largely shared this belief. After two days, the old witch doctor had done about all the business he could do, and the villagers were tired of feeding him. It was time for him to leave.

Azaan's wife was cooking outside over a wood fire. Her cast iron pot hung by a chain from a sturdy steel tripod over a low fire. The meal was mostly vegetables from her garden with some fish from one of Azaan's set lines. It simmered for hours filling the air with the pleasant smell of a hearty meal. The witch doctor came by often, acting as though he hoped to be invited for dinner. Late in the afternoon, when the pot was unattended, he passed closely and appeared to drop something into it. Kitafe saw him do it and so did two other boys. They finally had something to report to the old man and they were quickly off to find him.

That evening, as Azaan's family, Kitafe and the old man prepared to eat, Azaan called to the witch doctor and invited him to join them for dinner. Since he was always eating someone else's food, they were all surprised when he refused. The old man was not surprised.

"Come, I insist, we have plenty," he called again, but the witch doctor, thinking that maybe he'd been found out, said he was not hungry and must be leaving. As the strange little man headed quickly back down the trail with his scant possessions, toward where he had come from, Morgan said to the others, "Do not eat the food." He then took a spoonful and threw it at a nearby chicken. The bird hurried over to this rare bonanza and greedily ate it all before any of the other chickens noticed. In five minutes, the chicken lay dead. "That man was sent by Chao to kill me, but Kitafe and the boys saw him put the poison in the pot and told me. Please know, I do not want Chou to know the results of the little witch doctor's mission."

The old tracker walked directly to Azaan's hut, picked up his newly sharpened spear, thrust the thick assagi into his belt under his loose-fitting robe, and headed into the gathering darkness. He glided swiftly and noiselessly down the trail, rapidly closing the distance between him and the fleeing witch doctor.

When Azaan arose from his sleeping mat the next morning, he found his father sitting on a log, in front of last night's cooking fire, calmly smoking his pipe. "I do not think we will be seeing the little witch doctor again," Morgan said, "but I suspect we will soon be seeing Yazid."

CHAPTER 31

A WAY OUT

Chao had always hated Africa and everything about it. Africa was a culture he could not begin to understand—the food was poor, the wine and whiskey were worse, just taking a bath in a suspended canvas tub was a challenge, and there were no women to his liking. He was well paid, but due to sheer boredom, he managed to gamble much of it away. He desperately longed to return home, to friends, familiar food and pretty, sweet-smelling women, a house of his own. But to escape black Africa, he needed a lot more money than he currently had. He needed a quick, big score, and thoughts of the massive tusks of Huto were constantly on his mind and in his dreams. Even just one of those tusks could get him out of Africa and on his way to the familiar culture that raised him.

Escaping-Africa schemes dominated his thinking. With the fast boat and some criminally inclined Indian traders in Mozambique, he felt certain he could sell ivory for his own account easily cutting out the Asian trading company who employed him. After a couple more days of deliberation, he had a plan. He did not trust the little witch doctor who claimed that he could poison a person as he had done several times before. Chao paid him only half of the price he demanded and promised to pay the other half when the job was competed. When the would-be assassin did not return after several days, Chao was faced with several options; maybe the little scoundrel had simply fled with the money, particularly if he had heard that Chao had not paid the young elephant hunters, or maybe he was still at the village. Also, he had heard from the now-one-handed man about Morgan's deft use of his spear and wondered if the little man had been found out and paid the price.

He would send Yazid to the village for whatever game and fish he could buy. But mainly he wanted Yazid to find out what had happened to his hired killer. Then, he wanted Yazid to visit the young hunters downstream. He was to give them some money for the first elephant hunt and promise them more if they would help him hunt Huto. Chao knew that he should be the hunter; Yazid had already demonstrated his poor shooting ability and neither of the boys had ever shot the heavy rifle.

On the fourth day after the witch doctor's departure, Yazid docked the dugout below Azaan's village. Chao had taken the powerboat downriver on an unexplained mission. Although the water level was low and the current fairly slow at this time of the year, it was a six-mile paddle upstream against the current and Yazid was hot, tired and sullen. He quickly sought out Azaan and his father and explained Chao's plans as far as he knew them. Villagers drifted by slowly, trying to capture threads of the conversation. All of them had some idea of what probably befell the little witch doctor as young boys are generally poor at keeping a secret. Yazid knew that the witch doctor had spent time in the village but could only guess at his real mission. The demeanor of Azaan and the old man and later that of the villagers told him all he needed to know even though the little man was never mentioned. He could not completely rule it out, but he did not sense any current danger to Azaan or the old man.

The four-mile paddle downstream to the young hunters was much easier and Yazid arrived in his usual good humor. The boys were still making a limited effort at trapping and delivered a big wildebeest bull. Yazid paid them for it, and then paid them more for their part in the elephant hunt. Their faces told Yazid what he already knew; they were not paid nearly enough.

Then, he told them that Chao was nearly desperate to shoot the big bull with the heavy ivory that he had twice glimpsed along the south bank of the river. The boys glanced at each other and one said to Yazid, "This would be very dangerous. The bull you wish to shoot is now with a herd of cows that includes three young calves. Not only is the bull dangerous in the thick river brush, but the cows are ferocious in their defense of the little ones. I do not think that I want to be part of this." "Nor I," said his partner. The boys fear of hunting the elephant in the dense cover surprised Yazid, but then he remembered, "Chao wants to be the shooter;

you only need to get him to the elephants." This cast a different light on the hunt, even though it could, and probably would, be highly dangerous in the dense riverine reeds and brush. The boys had been watching the herd intermittently for several weeks, often from perches in the low-branched trees. They nodded at each other and the older one said, "Yazid, we will lead him to them, but we will not be part of the final stalk. By the time that occurs, we will be watching from the trees. Also, we do not trust Chao. He will need to pay us half before the hunt begins." Yazid smiled and said, "I will tell him." "Do not bring the powerboat, Yazid. The noise of the motor would spook them if they are close to where we meet. Come in two days in the morning. The heavy rains are surely coming soon."

Although the young hunters were nineteen or twenty years old, they realized that they had gotten themselves into a most serious situation. They were young, proud, and self-reliant but they could not see beyond what the consequence would be if Chao were to kill Huto. They both knew it was time to return to the village for the guidance of the elders. And they were homesick and most tired of their own poor cooking.

"What do you advise, honored one?" asked the older boy after explaining the planned hunt to Azaan and his father. Morgan sat quietly, contemplating the current situation in the context of the last two months, but particularly in the context of what he thought the future could hold. "I would not like to see that fine old elephant shot, and I would like to see Chao and his kind forever gone from this region. We all know that he is a clever and suspicious man, but he is also a greedy and ruthless one. Perhaps we can make the latter two characteristics work against him. Note how his cruel greed has alienated the villagers, you young hunters totally distrust him, and Yazid was appalled at his ruthlessness when Chao told him to kill me. He appears to be without friends or allies except perhaps in the big camp, but my guess would be that he has few friends anywhere. He has little or no moral conscience." He paused, slowly packed his pipe, and waited for a comment.

The older boy said, "We can easily steer him away from the big bull on this hunt, but he will keep trying as long as he is able." A collective hum rose from the men as they homed in on "as long as he is able."

"Killing him would put us in the same evil character mold as him," the old man said. "It would be on each of our consciences forever. Let us try to think of a way to make him have to or want to leave the area. Perhaps something natural that requires medical attention, maybe a fall or an accident or a wound, a snake bite, a broken bone. But how would we arrange that?"

To Morgan's great surprise, the younger of the hunters said, "I have an idea. Why don't you leave that matter to us?" The old man was at first skeptical, but the seriousness of this young man quickly convinced him. Neither he nor Azaan asked for any details. This job was strictly on a need-to-know basis.

CHAPTER 32

CONSEQUENCES

Njeri, Bahati and the breeding herd were last seen by the two young hunters about a mile upstream from their little camp and somewhat back away from the river. Some of the bushes had greened up quickly after the few brief showers. Huto prowled the edges of the little herd, greeting old lady friends and acting like the big, old gentleman that he usually was. Game trails traversed the brush beneath the taller trees and antelopes were everywhere.

Downstream, Chao prepared for the hunt. He cleaned and oiled the .375. He gently polished the soft tip of the cartridges. Although he did not hunt often, he liked guns, especially the heavy rifles, and he was a decent shot. He knew the shooting would be at close range, so he removed the scope from the gun. To avoid tangling up in the dense undergrowth, he also took off the strap. He'd make Yazid carry the heavy gun until they got close. Loaded, the rifle held three shells. Chao would carry four more, each in a separate pocket to keep them from clanging against each other. Midday in October in the Zambezi valley was sweltering hot, calling for short sleeves and short pants, no underwear. He knew that quiet stalking would be absolutely vital and wore thin soled low tennis shoes and no socks. He wore no bug spray or suntan lotion because of their odor. A camo ballcap concluded his careful preparations.

Chao, of course, did not help Yazid paddle the heavy dugout up to the hunters' camp. They arrived late in the morning with a hot sweaty Yazid staring up at thick, low storm clouds and hating Chao. Chao handed each of the young hunters the equivalent of five hundred American dollars, a huge amount in this place. But the boys knew the tusks would be worth at least fifty thousand American dollars, possibly even one hundred thousand American dollars. The young hunters quickly explained the herd was only about a mile upstream, but back in heavy cover away from the river. They recommended that Chao and Yazid wait until the little herd, hopefully with the big bull Huto, came to water later in the afternoon. There the undergrowth was thinner, and the hunter could watch a wide game trail as the animals passed and pick his quarry in a relatively open area. Chao was impatient but agreed to wait until late afternoon. Dark clouds were lowering, and the red orb of the setting sun was calling them as they set out. The younger hunter would paddle the dugout upstream to gather them up after the hunt.

The riverside trail was wide, well used and dusty. Occasional patches of dry leaves mixed with innumerable animal tracks. Chao easily recognized the unmistakable tracks of elephants and saw where a thick rock python had drug his heavy body through the dust. What he did not notice as unusual was a smooth, trackless area directly in front of them. The young hunter who was leading them seemed to stumble and fall to the side of the trail. Chao continued hurrying ahead down the center of the trail and onto the untracked area. The ground seemed to erupt as he stepped on the pan of a buried trap. The big leg-hold trap had been fashioned from the leaf spring of a truck and it literally jumped from the ground. It caught Chao's ankle where the long part of his shin met the flat top of his foot. Small bones shattered and the carrion-leaden jaw cut a shallow gash across this ankle. The other jaw of the trap snapped his Achilles tendon. In the gathering darkness, Chao knew that he was in most serious trouble. As he contemplated his situation and weighed his options, he realized that he had been set up; the young hunter had immediately disappeared into the darkness; Yazid would be his only friend.

Yazid helped him, nearly carried him, to the river and was both pleased and surprised to see in the gloom that the dugout was where they had left it. He was not surprised that the other hunter was also gone.

It was a terrifyingly slow, two-hour run in the dim light of a new moon, to the big poacher camp. Chao needed quick emergency attention, which awaited five hours downstream by the fast boat. But as Chao and Yazid rounded the last bend approaching camp, they saw that both the tarped cargo boat and the powerboat were adrift in the mile-wide river calmly drifting eastward on their way toward Mozambique. The dugout could never catch them. Yazid smiled grimly as he considered his own situation.

Even though he disliked everything about Chao, Yazid felt that he must help him. He called from the dugout and two sleepy, unhappy workers helped him get Chou to his surprisingly well-appointed, canvas tent. They dropped him roughly on his cot and shuffled off, muttering low curses. Yazid lit the gas lantern, pulled off Chao's bloody shoe, pulled a sheet over him and left to find him some water and whatever there was in camp to treat his cut and broken foot.

What was once a well-stocked first aid kit had been carelessly raided many times during the two months of the camp's existence. And little of value remained. Yazid found the remains of a bottle of antiseptic, a couple of small bandages, some aspirin, and a vial of penicillin, but no syringes. He cleaned the cut on the top of Chou's foot as best he could and poured the rest of the antiseptic into it. But it was a long cut with ragged edges and Yazid knew he had not done a very good repair job. He knew that infection was likely from the rotten skin and flesh on the jaws of the trap.

Next morning, using the small axe that they had used to remove the tusk from the elephant that he had shot two weeks earlier, Yazid was able to fashion a pair of crude crutches. Chao was able to get around the camp and, for the time being, could take care of himself. The camp was well stocked with food and Chao had an additional private stash of delicacies and whiskey. When Yazid had laid him on his cot the previous night, it was the first time anyone else had been in Chao's tent.

As the two men sipped from large cups of dark tea Yazid said, "I will take the dugout downstream to search for the powerboat.

The river level is low, and I think eventually the boat will run aground, probably on one of the many sand bars. I must do it now because as soon as the heavy rains begin, all the feeder streams will fill, and the river will rise quickly and carry the boats much farther downstream. I do not trust the men in camp, but you have the rifle. You must be strong; if you show any weakness, they will immediately take advantage. Do not let any of them get close to you."

Yazid packed the bare essentials, a little food, his big knife, an extra paddle and two five-gallon cans of gas. As he pushed off into the current, he was calm but apprehensive. What if the heavy rains came before he found the boat? What if he couldn't find the boat; with the rising water level and heavy current, he would not be able to paddle the heavy dugout back upstream to the poacher's camp, much less to Azaan's village.

On the third day, Yazid drifted past the tarped cargo boat. It was floating freely in a slow-swirling back-eddy where it would remain until the river level rose at least a couple of feet. The pungent smell of smoked meat from under a hot cover carried for another mile or more downstream. He hoped that sometime later he could return with some help and salvage the big motor.

On the fifth day, twenty some miles downstream, he found the powerboat. It had drifted onto a mid-river sand bar and as the river level had recently dropped a few inches, the boat was solidly anchored in the loose sand. But now, Yazid was stymied; the boat was far too heavy for him to pull or push out into the current. Even the 50-horsepower engine was too heavy to move. So, the savvy river boatman sat on the captain's seat, lit his pipe and calmly considered his options. The sand was clearly too soft to use rollers. But then it hit him; if the sand was that soft, it should be easy to dig. He could dig around and under it and float it out into the river. The paddles were good digging tools in the loose sand and in two steamy hours of digging and pushing sand away, the powerboat floated freely.

While he dug, Yazid had watched a noisy, slow-moving thunderstorm approach from the west, along the south bank of the river. A few big drops hit him as he transferred gear and gas cans from the dugout to the powerboat. He would tow the dugout behind, although he didn't know exactly why he was saving the heavy, clumsy thing now that he had the fast powerboat; perhaps it was because it had been his father's boat.

The slow-moving storm had locally dropped copious amounts of rain. One of the dry sand riverbeds that Yazid had noticed as he searched for the boats was now swollen to the bank tops. The thick, brown stream thundered through everything in its path, carrying entire uprooted trees, burned logs, animal carcasses. As the rainy season progressed, Yazid knew that these debris laden tributaries would make the Zambezi a most dangerous place for all boats, large and small.

CHAPTER 33

THE PASSING

The long, slow ride up the river; towing the heavy dugout, dodging the occasional partially sunken log and steering around hippo pods had delivered Yazid back at the poacher camp late in the afternoon. The camp seemed unusually quiet as he tied both boats to the roots of an ancient tree. He was used to the noise of the generator, the portable radios and the voices of the men. When he topped the riverbank, he immediately noticed a large, dark form on the grass close to Chao's tent, and soon realized that it was a man, a dead man. The man was the leader of Chao's work crew.

Chou was sitting on his cot with his bare leg propped on a stool. Yazid immediately saw that the leg was extremely swollen and red streaks run from his ankle, up the pale leg and disappeared beneath his white shorts. Without speaking, Yazid laid the back of his hand against Chao's face. The man had a raging fever but was lucid.

"What happened?" Yazid asked, pointing at the dead man.

"Three days ago, the men came to my tent and wanted my money," Chao gasped. "I told them no, but I knew they would come back and later that day they did. I expected them and had buried my money. The rifle was under my sheet. As I believe you advised, I shot the leader before they could get close to me. The others are gone but left him lying there. They took the old Johnboat but there was very little gas."

Chao had dressed himself all in white; it was his funeral attire. He asked Yazid to dig a burial hole just outside the tent. Yazid agreed but wondered, "Why there?"

By noon the next day, Chao was dead. Yazid knew that he could not bury him beside his tent; scavenging animals would quickly find the body and dig it out of the ground. It slowly occurred to Yazid why maybe he had saved the old dugout. He carefully dragged Chao's body down to the water's edge and wrapped the white-clad body in a fresh white sheet. Chao's pillow was retrieved from the tent and his body was gently laid in the old boat. Yazid then pushed the dugout quietly into the current and watched it until it drifted around a bend and out of sight. Although the man was not his friend, the finality of his passing sent a shiver down Yazid's back. Yazid wanted to be anywhere else. He wanted to be with his friends.

CHAPTER 34

A NEW HOME

As he motored slowly upriver toward Azaan's village, he saw the big elephant, Huto, standing completely exposed on a sandy beach. The massive tusks gleamed in the morning sun and his wet skin seemed nearly black. With the poaching business firmly behind him, Yazid now surveyed Huto for the magnificent specimen he was, rather than solely for the enormous value of his tusks. For some reason unknown to him, Yazid waved as he passed. A mile farther upstream, the matriarch and her herd were just leaving the water and crossing a white sand beach, heading for the shade of the tall trees. He paused midstream to watch; the three littlest ones ran to keep up with the walking pace of the adults.

It was a peaceful scene that caused him to smile and think about what would become his new life.

Azaan's wife had a widowed sister who lived in the village with a seven-year-old son. Her name was Chiriki and she had been alone for four years. When he was a trader, Yazid had noticed that Chiriki had a small boy, but did not seem to have a man. He had never spoken to her, but they had exchanged glances and small smiles. Yazid wanted her to be part of his new life, as a farmer, as a father, as a newly minted person of respect. As a woman without a man, Azaan, the brother-in-law, would act in the role of her guardian. Thoughts of her dominated as he climbed the bank into the village, but first he must tell Azaan, the old man and the villagers of the happenings downriver and of Chao and the poachers.

The two young hunters had returned to their homes in the village the morning after Chao stepped on the trap but had told no one of the incident. Yazid detailed the aftermath of the trap catching Chao's foot but did not say that it had been deliberately set to injure him, injure him sufficiently to require out-of-country medical care. Most of the villagers assumed it was simply an accident.

After the many questions, the old man stood and began, "Let us put this all behind us. This was an evil person. He tried to have me and Kitafe and Azaan's whole family poisoned; he attempted to kidnap Kitafe, and he made some inroads into corrupting many of you. For reasons obvious to all of us, I think it best if we do not report any of this to the authorities. We can deal with any unresolved issues ourselves." A mental sigh of relief passed through the two hunters and several other village men. A blinding flash of lightning and a nearly simultaneous clap of thunder sent everyone running to cover. Yazid had nowhere to go; as he prepared for a cold drenching; then, Chiriki caught his eye and nodded toward her small place.

The first heavy shower in many months cleared the air of dust and smoke and a brilliantly clear, warm morning drew nearly everyone outside. Since most of the villagers were close enough to hear, Azaan began in a loud voice, "When Chao tried to convince you to poach for him, he offered tobacco, whiskey, radios, flashlights and so forth. When my father objected, Chao said, 'Don't you want them to have a better life?' And my father said that a better life was not tobacco and whiskey, but perhaps access to medical treatment; therefore, a boat, a generator, organized schooling, and for him, properly cured pipe tobacco." As he spoke, the people gathered round, wondering what this little speech was leading to. "Chao is dead, the poachers are gone, but the camp remains. This afternoon Yazid, my father and I will go down to it in the powerboat and salvage what we can use here."

It was a sparse remainder of the camp that Azaan and Morgan had scouted months before; little remained. Yazid explained that the tarped cargo boat had been loaded for its last downriver run with much of the camp gear, prior to the coming rains, and the fleeing poachers would have grabbed what they could carry.

"Let us take the generator, coolers, folding camp chairs and all the filled gas cans," said Azaan, "and Yazid is there a chainsaw, and can you find the store of tobacco my father is so fond of?"

As they finished loading the powerboat, the old man asked Yazid, "Where did Chao want you to dig his burial hole?"

Yazid pointed to the tent and said, "Right beside the north wall of his tent. I don't know why."

"Maybe I do," replied Morgan. In Chao's tent the heavy rifle leaned against one inside corner beside a small wooden table. His cot now held a thin pad and a sheet and sat on a reed mat against the north wall. Morgan slid the cot away from the wall and lifted the mat. Beneath where his head would have lain was an area of fresh dirt. "If you dig there, I believe that you will find his money. Some Orientals like to be close to their money when they die." Chao was apparently one of them.

Yazid and Azaan would return the following day to pick up the generator and gas cans. They would burn the meat cutting tables, the smoking racks, tents, pads, everything, knowing that the forest would slowly reclaim that which rightfully belonged to it.

As Yazid cruised by the elephants, on the way to his new home, he thought he could hear a lion roaring in the distance.

CHAPTER 35

A VISIT

Although the riverside villages are widely separated, news seems to flow easily. So, it was no surprise to Azaan and Morgan when Federal Rangers appeared at the village a week or so after the burning of the poacher camp. The Rangers had heard reports of a tall smoke plume, troubling news in this still-dry land. The rangers had come from their post far downriver, and therefore saw and inspected the abandoned cargo boat loaded with rapidly decomposing meat.

Villagers far downstream had seen the smoke and reported it, but they were unaware of the cargo boat. The rangers correctly suspected that better information would probably be found upstream in Azaan's village.

Morgan was pleased to see two old friends among the four Rangers. Since they had seen the cargo boat and the burned camp, the rangers pretty much knew what the current situation was: no fire, no poacher camp and no poachers, but wondered how it all came to be. After a couple of hours of quiet talk, polite indirect talk with no hard questions and no accusations or denials, the rangers understood most of what had transpired. They would take no action: the remaining poachers were probably in Mozambique and no crime was revealed among the villagers. The body of Chao in the old dugout was not seen, and therefore not mentioned and two fine ivory tusks had mysteriously disappeared. Also, politely not mentioned was the fast power boat, anchored just upstream.

One of Morgan's Ranger friends asked when he and the boy planned to leave; the heavy rains would soon arrive, and a four day walk in the rain would be miserable. Then, he smiled and said, "Look Morgan, why don't you and the boy ride with us down the river to our post. In a day or two, we will be driving some of our seasonal workers out to their home village, which is close to yours. You both could ride out with them. And, thinking ahead, if you wanted to, next year you and Kitafe could come back to Azaan's village by way of the truck when we pick up the workers, and then take the boat up the river. It would all happen in a day."

The boy and his grandfather could not stop smiling.